320.6 G369
Gerken, Heather K., 1969-
The democracy index : why
our election system is
failing and how to fix it
67025

WITHDRAWN

THE
DEMOCRACY
INDEX

320.6
G369

HEATHER K. GERKEN

Princeton University Press
Princeton and Oxford

067025

Copyright © 2009 by Princeton University Press

Requests for permission to reproduce material from this work should be sent to Permissions, Princeton University Press

Published by Princeton University Press, 41 William Street, Princeton, New Jersey 08540

In the United Kingdom: Princeton University Press, 6 Oxford Street, Woodstock, Oxfordshire OX20 1TW

All Rights Reserved

Library of Congress Cataloging-in-Publication Data

Gerken, Heather K., 1969–

The democracy index : why our election system is failing and how to fix it / Heather K. Gerken.

p. cm.

Includes bibliographical references and index.

ISBN 978-0-691-13694-3 (hardcover : alk. paper) 1. Voting—United States.

2. Elections—United States. 3. Voter registration—United States. I. Title.

JK1976.G47 2008

320.60973—dc22

2008047802

British Library Cataloging-in-Publication Data is available

This book has been composed in Adobe Garamond pro

Printed on acid-free paper. ∞

press.princeton.edu

Printed in the United States of America

1 3 5 7 9 10 8 6 4 2

For my remarkable parents

Contents

Acknowledgments

A few years ago, the Tobin Project asked me to pull together a group of scholars to explore the ways in which our work connected to ongoing policy debates. Academics have become increasingly distant from the world of policy, and our goal was to rebuild the ties that once existed between scholars and lawmakers. During our first meeting, I challenged the scholars to present a genuinely "modest proposal," a small-scale intervention that would improve the way our democracy works. That's where I first presented my idea for a Democracy Index. At the time, I thought that the idea would take up a few days and a bit of ink. Instead, it caught hold, and I've spent a good chunk of the last eighteen months thinking and writing about it. Shortly after I published an editorial on the idea in the *Legal Times*, Senators Barack Obama and Hillary Clinton each put the idea into proposed legislation. Within the year, Congress set aside $10 million to fund model data-collection programs in five states, and several foundations—including the Pew Center on the States—funded conferences and initial research on the idea. All of this activity prompted me to write this book, which makes the case for creating the Index and offers my own take on how it should be designed.

I am deeply indebted to Michael Caudell-Feagan, Doug Chapin, Ned Foley, John Fortier, and Paul Gronke, along with their staff at the Pew Center on the States, electionline, the Moritz College of Law at Ohio State, AEI/Brookings, and Reed College's Early Voting Information Center. They all worked tirelessly to shape the proposal and move it toward reality, offering advice, financial support, and organizational muscle to push the idea forward. I wouldn't have made it past the editorial stage without them. I owe great thanks to the people who patiently read the entire draft: Bruce Ackerman, Doug Chapin, Ned Foley, Barry Gerken, Thad Hall, Michael Kang, Justin Levitt, Ben Sachs, David Schleicher, Dan Tokaji, three anonymous reviewers, and my editor at Princeton, Chuck Myers, and copy editor Richard Isomaki. Over the course of the last eighteen months, I have also received helpful comments from Ian Ayres, Kim Brace, Richard Brooks, Kareem Crayton, Chris Elmendorf, Dan Esty, Deborah Goldberg, Rick Hasen, Steve Huefner, Christine Jolls, Katerina Linos, Jerry Mashaw, Michael McDonald, Rick Pildes, Charles Stewart, and Jonathan Zittrain; the staff and advisers who helped Senator Barack Obama put the idea into pending legislation; the faculty of Oklahoma City University Law School; and audience members at the Section on Legislation session at the 2007 meeting of the Association of American Law Schools. I've benefited greatly from the thoughts and criticisms offered by the participants in the Designing a Democracy Index conference sponsored by the Pew Center on the States, the Joyce Foundation, and the Mortiz College of Law; the participants in the 2007 Academics' Conference sponsored by the AEI-Brookings Election Reform Project; and the participants in the Data for Democracy Conference sponsored by the Pew Charitable Trusts and the JEHT Foundation. I am especially grateful for the many reformers, academics and election officials (including three secretaries of state) who took time from their busy schedules to talk to me about the work they do. You will see their names scattered throughout the book. Thanks also to David Pervin for suggesting I write this book and to the Tobin Project for pushing me to think about this project in the first place. I am grateful for the financial support provided by the Oscar M. Ruebhausen Fund and the Yale Law School and the assistance provided by Theresa Cullen and the staff of the Yale Law Library. Scott Grinsell, Sarah Burg, Jill Habig, Dina Mishra, John Nann, Ari Weisbard, Saumya Manohar, William Rinner, and Marin Levy provided excellent research support. I must give special thanks to Manav Bhatnagar, who did the bulk of the research and responded to all requests with exceptional speed and good cheer, and to Scott Grinsell, who patently read through an early draft. Peter Miller provided invaluable help in putting together the ranking of state disclosures, and Daniel Bowen was very helpful in assessing initial measurement processes. Finally, thanks to my husband, David Simon, who makes all things possible and who would blush if I wrote what he means to me.

Introduction:

Why We Need a Democracy Index

Our election system is run badly. Although many people are aware of the problem and eager for a solution, reform efforts have gotten surprisingly little traction. This book explains why election reform has yet to catch hold and offers a promising new solution for getting change passed: a "Democracy Index," which would rank states and localities based on how their election systems perform.

THE PROBLEM

The best evidence we have suggests that our election system is clunky at best and dysfunctional at worst.* Ballots are discarded. Poll workers are poorly trained. Registration lists work badly. Lines can be too long. Machines malfunction. Partisan officials change the rules of the game to help themselves and hurt their enemies. Election administrators cannot agree on what constitutes a best practice, or even whether there is any such thing. Authority is decentralized, so it's hard to know who's to blame when a problem occurs. Most experts agree that the system we use to run our elections is chronically underfunded, often poorly run, and sometimes administered in a partisan fashion.

*Rather than repeat the phrase "the best evidence we have" in every other sentence of this book, let me offer a general caveat about the diagnoses offered here. As chapter 2 makes clear, it is difficult to make precise claims about the current state of the election system because the data are so sparse. What I describe here are the symptoms that experts routinely see and the field's best guesses as to their root causes. These assessments are based on the best information available, but better information would be necessary to state these claims with certainty. One of the main points of the book is that we should be deeply troubled by our inability to know whether the system is working or not.

People assume that the fiascos we saw in Florida in 2000 and Ohio in 2004 are outliers, crises caused by a level of partisanship and mismanagement that does not exist elsewhere. Partisanship and mismanagement surely played a role in those debacles. But both states were also in the wrong place at the wrong time, victims of a turnout tsunami that too few states are equipped to handle. A crisis is not around every bend in the United States. But that's only because elections usually aren't close enough for these routine problems to affect the outcome. Unless we fix the underlying causes, debacles can occur almost anywhere.

In 2006, a hotly contested congressional race took place in Florida. The margin of victory? 373 votes. The number of people who went into the voting booth but did not cast a ballot that counted? 18,000.[1] A malfunctioning computer in Carteret County, North Carolina, lost 4,400 votes during the 2004 election, with no means of recovering them.[2] The same year poll workers in Orange County, California, gave the wrong ballots to 7,000 people in a primary election, a mistake that may have affected the results in several races.[3] During a 2006 primary, election workers in Maryland forgot the cards they needed to start up the election machinery. More than 200 precincts could not open until late morning.[4] That same year, a group of computer scientists discovered it was surprisingly easy to steal votes by inserting a virus into the electronic voting machines used by 10 percent of Americans.[5] In Colorado, long lines at polling places deterred about 20,000 people from voting, 20 percent of expected turnout.[6] A subsequent review largely blamed Colorado's new software, which was "of decidedly sub-professional architecture and construction and appears never to have been tested in any meaningful manner."[7] That's expert speak for "tut, tut, tut."

Cuyahoga County, Ohio, is probably lucky that MSNBC's Keith Olbermann doesn't choose a "worst election system in the world." Problems seem to occur every cycle. After suffering the long lines and chaos that afflicted many Ohio counties in 2004, Cuyahoga denizens opened their morning papers to read headlines like "Election Staff Convicted in Recount Rig."[8] In May 2006, election workers lost 70 computer memory cards containing voting records, 15,000 absentee ballots had to be hand-counted because the machines could not read them, and numerous polling problems occurred. It took five days to report the results.[9] All of this led Ohio's new secretary of state, Jennifer Brunner, to demand the resignations of the entire board.[10] But problems persist. In November 2007, the server used to count votes repeatedly froze and crashed.[11] Worse, administrators discovered that "20 percent of the printouts from touch-screen voting machines were unreadable and had to be reprinted."[12] All of this might be quite funny—a local government version of *The Office*—if election results weren't riding on it. "God help us," said one county official, if the next presidential race "depend[s] on Cuyahoga County."[13]

At first glance, it looks like reform ought to be easy to pass in the United States. There's a good deal of agreement that we have a problem and a myriad of proposals for solving it. Not a week goes by without someone issuing a report or proposing a change. In 2007, close to one hundred reform bills were circulated in Congress, with more than nineteen hundred proposed in state legislatures. Hundreds of academic articles addressed reform issues. Dozens of good-governance groups offered hundreds of reports and proposals on their websites.

The political environment also seems receptive to change. Who, after all, is against democracy working better? One suspects that the word *democratic* is routinely appended to policy proposals only because it conveys more gravitas than "motherhood" or "apple pie."

Finally, the fiascos we've seen in recent years should have provided a powerful impetus for change. Reform is a notoriously crisis-driven industry. It is always tough to get anything on the legislative agenda. But "electoral meltdowns"[14] have been a regular occurrence in recent years. Just ask any academic who specializes in elections. Many of us have moved from laboring in obscurity to serving as commentators on CNN. Like a plague of tweed-clad cicadas, we return from academic hibernation every couple of years to feed on whatever election controversy is brewing.

Despite all of this, serious reform has not yet gotten traction in this country. Even in the wake of the 2000 fiasco—which made the United States an international laughing stock—all Congress could do was pass the relatively toothless Help America Vote Act. The Act has helped us make genuine progress in several areas, as I explain in the next chapter. But it addressed only the symptoms of the Florida debacle, not its root causes: inadequate funding, amateur staffing, and partisanship.

Just think about that for a moment. There's a strong consensus that we have a problem, lots of potential solutions, a reform community ready to act, and a cause that voters support. Yet even a crisis like the 2000 election prompted only modest reform. If that's not a sign that we need a new approach to reform, I don't know what is.

WHY WE HAVEN'T FIXED THE PROBLEM

Why hasn't reform gotten much traction in the United States? Partisanship and localism generate political tides that run against change. Unlike most developed democracies, state and local officials run our elections, leading to what one scholar has termed "hyper-decentralization."[15] Worse, many of those local officials have strong partisan ties. This unusual combination of partisanship and localism not only results in a poorly run system, but makes change hard to come by. At worst, election officials administer elections in a partisan or unprofessional fashion. At best, they have few incentives to invest in the system and lots of reasons to resist change. These factors combine to stymie reform.

Unfortunately, voters and reformers have been unable to alter this perverse political dynamic. Voters have only a haphazard sense of how well elections are run, and no comparative data that would tell them which systems work and which don't. We do not even know how many people *cast a ballot* during our last presidential election,[16] let alone how well our election system is performing. Voters learn that there's a problem only when an election is so close that the outcome is in doubt. That's like measuring annual rainfall by counting how often lightning strikes.

Reformers similarly struggle in today's political environment. Even when lightning strikes—when there's a crisis that could energize a coalition for change—debates about reform quickly descend into highly technical arguments that voters have no yardstick for judging. Even when reformers manage to get policymakers' attention, they lack the information they need to make a credible case for change. Reformers work hard to overcome these obstacles, but most ask policymakers to ignore their self-interest and do the right thing. Little wonder that reform hasn't yet gotten much traction.

The dilemma is clear. While the basic ingredients for change exist—a national consensus that there's a problem, an active reform community, an intuitively popular cause, and semiregular crises to place the issue on the agenda—political incentives create a drag on reform efforts. The problem is hardly insurmountable. If reformers can persuade legislators to restore the voting rights of felons,[17] improving our election system is surely a cause with political legs. But we need to align the incentives of politicians with the interests of voters on this issue. We need to give local officials a reason to pay attention. We need a new approach to election reform.

A NEW APPROACH

This book offers a new approach. It argues that we should create a Democracy Index that ranks states and localities based on election performance. The Index would function as the rough equivalent of the *U.S. News and World Report* rankings for colleges and graduate schools.* It would focus on issues that matter to all voters: how long did you spend in line? how many ballots were discarded? how often did voting machines break down? The Index would tell voters not only whether things are working in their own state, but how their state compares to its neighbors.

The Democracy Index is unusual because it works with political incentives, not against them. By providing the right information in the right form, it has the potential to create an environment that is receptive to change. It is a data-driven, information-forcing device designed to generate pressure for reform while helping us make more sensible choices about which reforms to pursue.

First, the Democracy Index pulls together the right information: comparative data on state and local performance. Comparative data on bottom line results should reveal problems that haphazard data conceal, helping us pinpoint solutions and make the case for change. Today reformers and

*This sentence might not inspire confidence in those familiar with the foolishness the *U.S. News and World Report* rankings have engendered. As I explain in chapters 2 and 4, however, the Index addresses easily quantifiable, nuts-and-bolts issues that lend themselves to quantitative measurement in a way that educational quality does not. Moreover, while "teaching to the test" is always a worry for any ranking, a well-designed Democracy Index is a good deal better than having no test at all.

election officials argue incessantly about which direction we should go. But no one has a map that tells us where we are now. Comparative data would give us that map.

Second, the Index packages the data in the right form: it *ranks* states and localities against one another. By distilling performance data into a highly accessible form, the Index gives voters a rough sense of how well their system is doing, precisely the information they need to call election officials to account. A ranking should work for the simplest of reasons: no one wants to be at the bottom of the list.

Because the Democracy Index provides the right information in the right form, it should harness the two major obstacles to reform—partisanship and localism—in the service of reform. An Index would make election problems visible and concrete to voters and policymakers alike. And it would give politicians a reason to care about how well the system is working.

Even if the Democracy Index failed to gin up political support for reform, it should still improve the handling of elections. We typically assume that voters and politicians alone can hold administrators accountable for their missteps. In many fields, however, bureaucrats police themselves based on shared professional norms. Peer pressure, it turns out, can be just as effective in the workplace as it is in high school. By providing a professional touchstone in the field, the Democracy Index could help generate a consensus on best practices, something sorely needed in election administration.

GETTING FROM HERE TO THERE IN ELECTION REFORM

While the book's central purpose is to make the case for a Democracy Index, it is animated by a larger theme. We have a "here to there" problem in election reform. We spend a great deal of time thinking about what's wrong with our election system (the "here") and how to fix it (the "there"). But we spend almost no time thinking about how to get from here to there—how to create an environment in which reform can actually take root. Reform advocates work tirelessly to help specific projects blossom. But they are fighting this battle on difficult terrain, and almost no one is thinking about how to change the terrain itself. We've spent too much time identifying the journey's end and not enough time figuring out how to smooth the road that leads there.

There is little point in continuing to fight the same fight in the vague hope that something will eventually take. We should take a step back and figure out how to create an environment that is more receptive to change generally. It is time to think less about the end game and more about the interim strategies and institutional tweaks that will help us get from here to there. The Democracy Index is just such a solution.

The "Here to There" Problem

The "here to there" problem is endemic in election reform circles. Scholarly proposals often have a "just add water" quality, as if merely announcing a good idea is enough to get it passed. The problem is perfectly captured by a *New Yorker* cartoon, with two professors poring over a complicated math problem. A simple notation explains the key step in the equation: "Then a miracle occurs." To be fair, some academics have thought hard about why reform is difficult to pass, with partisanship and localism being the usual suspects in most analyses. But phrases like "the perils of partisanship" or the "problem of localism" are usually punch lines to the story, not starting points for the analysis.

A handful of scholars have written sporadically about the here-to-there question.[18] Unlike scholars who specialize in areas like campaign finance or redistricting, however, we do not think of ourselves as addressing the same question or writing in the same field.[19] We haven't thought systematically about what connects our work to each other's or to the broader project of election reform.

This is surprising. After all, most arguments for election reform depend on a single premise: process shapes substance. Academics are quick to tell you that the structure of our political process (campaign finance law, redistricting rules) helps determine the substance of our policies (who gets elected, what gets passed). But they do not apply that lesson to election reform. The structure of our political process also determines what kind of election reform gets passed. Or, in the case of the United States, it creates an environment where precious little gets passed.

The here-to-there problem is not confined to the academy. Blue-ribbon panels and good-governance groups often propose overhauling our election system or enacting laundry lists of nuts-and-bolts proposals. Though reformers who labor in the political trenches are painfully aware that we cannot "just add water" to get change passed, most spend too much time describing the change they want and too little time thinking about fashioning a political environment that is receptive to it. Take a look at the final report of the Carter-Baker Commission,[20] the most high profile reform effort in recent years. It offers pages of detailed recommendations but says almost nothing about what we could do to ensure that at least some of these recommendations see the light of day.

Reformers, of course, spend a lot of time thinking about the here-to-there problem for specific projects. They work tirelessly to build support for this or that proposal—educating the public, lobbying officials, filing lawsuits. But good-governance groups lack the resources they need to grapple with the here-to-there problem writ large. That's because reformers are beholden to funders. And funders tend favor big over small, end goals over interim solutions, silver bullets over institutional tweaks, substantive proposals over procedural fixes. As one reform advocate ruefully told me, "Process is not sexy."[21] And the here-to-there question is process squared—changing the reform process to make more significant procedural reforms possible. For funders anxious to see concrete results—bills passed, reports issued, news articles written—"smoothing the path for election reform" looks like a nebulous project indeed.[22] The result is that the people who know the most about how the reform process works have the fewest opportunities to change it.

Solving the Here-to-There Problem

If the work of reformers is to be something other than a Sisyphean task, process should be our main focus, and smoothing the path for change ought to be at the top of the reform agenda. Here-to-there proposals may seem modest when compared to typical reform proposals, like calls for public financing or nonpartisan election administration. But these wide-ranging reform proposals have been met with a deafening silence. We have plenty of ideas about what kind of change we want. What we need is an environment in which change can happen.

The Democracy Index offers a quintessentially here-to-there solution. It does not create national performance standards. It does not take power away from partisan officials. It does not even endorse a set of best practices for administering elections. Instead, it pushes in the direction of better performance, less partisanship, and greater professionalism. The Index does so not by trying to resist the fierce push against change generated by our political system's twin engines—partisan warfare and local competition—but by harnessing partisanship and localism in the service of change. It is a modest reform that makes bigger, better reform possible. It gets us from here to there.

This book is organized as follows.

Chapter 1 canvasses the problems we see in our election system and identifies their root causes: partisanship and localism, which have produced a badly run system and stymied efforts to change it. The chapter argues that the first step toward meaningful reform is to reverse the political tides that have run so long against reform. A Democracy Index—described in some detail at the end of the chapter—represents one such solution.

Chapters 2 and 3 explain why the Democracy Index should alter the political incentives that too often prevent reform from getting traction. While most businesses and government agencies measure relentlessly, election administration—which is ripe for quantitative analysis—is a world without data. These chapters show how difficult it is to run an election system—let alone improve it—in a world without data. And they explain why a ranking system represents a particularly effective strategy for distilling election performance data and prodding election officials to improve. An Index should affect the three major leverage points in the reform process, giving voters the information they need to hold election officials accountable, putting pressure on policymakers to do the right thing, and helping administrators police themselves.

While a Democracy Index can correct the perverse political incentives that stymie reform, chapter 4 warns that it could also introduce different problems into the reform calculus. A poorly designed ranking might push states to compete along the wrong dimensions and create incentives for election administrators to cook the books. There are strategies for mitigating these problems, but these risks go hand in hand with the benefits associated with ranking, and it is important not to ignore them.

Chapter 5 considers the here-to-there question in miniature—how to make the Democracy Index a reality. This chapter first addresses the political question—whether the Democracy Index itself is likely to get traction. The proposal has already garnered significant attention from policymakers, academics, and foundations. It has been incorporated into separate legislation by Senators Hillary Clinton and Barack Obama. Congress has set aside ten million dollars to fund model data-collection efforts by the states. And several major foundations have already poured significant resources into the early stages of the Index's development. Nonetheless, as further detailed in this chapter, obstacles remain. Chief among them are collecting the necessary data and getting buy-in from election administrators. While there are reasons to be optimistic about the idea's future, even a modest proposal like this one will need some help along the way.

This chapter also returns to the question introduced in chapter 1—what should a Democracy Index look like? It details the challenges involved in creating one. Any effort to assemble it will involve what political scientist Paul Gronke calls a "pushmi-pullyu" process.* The designers of the Democracy Index will have to toggle between the ideal and the real—the things they want to measure and the data that actually exist—in determining what is ultimately included in the Index. This chapter suggests some creative strategies for obtaining the data we need and offers examples of the metrics the Index might include.

The book concludes by returning to the broader theme that animates it: how to get from "here to there" in election reform. The Democracy Index is part of a larger shift in reform circles. The new generation of reformers is moving away from top-down regulation to market-driven solutions. They eschew civil-rights rhetoric for data-driven policymaking. Unyielding in their idealism, they are pragmatic, even eclectic, in their approach. The concluding chapter notes that the Democracy Index offers some larger lessons about what drives reform and argues that the Index beats out most other reform proposals for a simple reason: it should help make those proposals a reality.

*One hopes that the process gets farther than did the magical creature in the Dr. Dolittle books.

1 The Perverse Politics of Election Reform

Why (We Think) Elections Are Run Badly, and What to Do about It

The best evidence available suggests that our election system suffers from the same problem that afflicts the nation's physical infrastructure: deferred maintenance. We have not invested enough resources in buying voting machines, designing polling places, training poll workers, and updating policies. Politics and localism are the root causes of these symptoms. These unusual features of the U.S. system not only undermine its quality, but thwart efforts to improve it. If we want to get from "here to there" in election reform, we must alter this perverse dynamic. One of the most promising strategies to do so is a Democracy Index.

THE PROBLEM

Deferred Maintenance

During the last few years, we've witnessed bridges collapsing, dams bursting, even a giant sinkhole in Portland that swallowed the truck sent to fix it.[1] These problems were all caused by a phenomenon long familiar to experts and bureaucrats: deferred maintenance, a phrase that made its way into national headlines when a bridge in Minnesota collapsed in 2007.[2] The phrase captures a simple idea: we aren't taking care of the nation's physical infrastructure.[3]

We aren't taking care of the nation's democratic infrastructure, either. It is made up of people instead of bridges, voting machines instead of highways, regulations instead of dams. The evidence of neglect can be seen across the country. Registration systems function badly. Voting machines break down. Poll workers are often poorly trained and badly compensated.[4] Too many ballots go uncounted because of bad ballot design or malfunctioning machinery. Eligible voters are sometimes turned away from the polls or leave in frustration because of long lines or hassles they encounter at the polling place.[5] Polling places can be hard to reach, poorly laid out, and in need of more parking.[6]

People describing this problem usually start with the 2000 presidential election.[7] Thousands of eligible voters were improperly purged from registration lists and denied a chance to vote. Thousands more appear to have voted for the wrong presidential candidate because of bad ballot design. Outdated voting machines prevented still more voters from casting a ballot that could be counted. While these problems can happen in any election, they mattered a great deal in a race with a 537-vote margin, where the outcome would determine our next president.

There is a danger, however, in starting any discussion about our election system with a story like Florida. Not every dam, bridge, or highway ramp is going to collapse. So, too, debacles like Florida's are not around every bend. That's why this chapter began by describing the problem as deferred maintenance, not outright crisis. Because most elections are won by large margins, votes discarded and voters deterred usually won't affect the outcome.

Nonetheless, if it's a mistake to conclude that the system is about to fall apart based on what occurred in Florida, it's also a mistake to conclude that things are working well in the many places where a crisis has not occurred. When elections are competitive—when lots of new voters want to register, when turnout is high, when elections are decided by a small margin—we put more pressure on our creaky system than it can bear. It is precisely when we care most about an election's outcome—when voters are energized and the race is hard fought—that we will be least confident about the results. It's tempting to say we are playing Russian roulette with our democracy. But that's the wrong metaphor; the odds of disaster aren't that steep. The problem is that we aren't prepared for the electoral equivalent of a Category 4 or 5 hurricane. The human costs of neglect are strikingly different in elections and hurricanes. But the metaphor captures both the predictability and unpredictability of problems that arise from deferred maintenance. It's hard to tell where disaster will strike, but it doesn't make sense to bet against disaster in the long haul. We can't all rely on what Rick Hasen terms "the election administrator's prayer: 'Lord, let this election not be close.'"[8]

The State of Our Election System

The introduction describes some of the specific problems associated with deferred maintenance. Statistics can offer a more systemic view, though they come with the same caveat I offered in the introduction: we don't have enough data to be sure of the diagnoses I offer below. We ought to be deeply embarrassed that the phrase "we think" had to be included in the title of this chapter.

What evidence we do have indicates that between one and a half and three million votes were lost solely because of problems with the registration process during the 2000 election, with several million more lost to other causes.[9] According to the 2000 U.S. census, about one million registered voters said that they did not vote because polling lines were too long or polling hours were too short.[10] In 2004, we were missing one-quarter of the two million poll workers needed to administer the election.[11] In 2006, 43 percent of local officials surveyed about the prior presidential election reported that an electronic voting system malfunctioned, with 11 percent reporting a breakdown that could not be fixed. Twenty-one percent of those officials reported that poll workers did not understand their jobs, and 10 percent had problems with poll workers failing to show up to work. Twelve percent admitted that there were "excessively long lines" on Election Day.[12]

The risks associated with deferred maintenance are especially high for the intensely competitive elections that have become commonplace in recent years. In 2000, it took us more than a month to figure out who would be president. In 2004, we were not that far from a similar disaster. Had the Electoral College count come down to New Mexico (where Bush won by only 6,000 votes) instead of Ohio (where Bush enjoyed a 135,000-vote margin),[13] we might have witnessed the same type of brouhaha that led Fidel Castro—admittedly not a man cursed with self awareness—to offer to send election monitors in 2000.[14] The same problems, minus the intervention of a puckish Cuban dictator, afflict state and local elections.

Washington's 2004 gubernatorial election took seven months to resolve and continues to generate bad will and conspiracy theories on both sides of the political aisle.[15]

Too Little Progress Made since 2000

While these problems are known to every seasoned politician–one scholar calls them "election administration's family secret"[16]—too little has been done to fix them. Some things got a good deal better in the wake of 2000, largely because of the Help America Vote Act (HAVA) passed by Congress in 2002.[17] HAVA provided much-needed funding for new voting machines and made some sensible adjustments to state balloting processes. The funding has been particularly important in replacing outdated technology, helping to reduce the number of ballots lost to machine problems.

Still, even these important reforms seem quite modest when compared to the crisis that prompted them. HAVA failed to create comprehensive national standards for running our elections. It failed to provide for adequate enforcement of the few standards it did set. It even failed to fund the agency it created to coordinate the act's new policies. As one AP report explains, two years after HAVA passed, the Election Assistance Commission it created "had no desks, no computers, and no office to put them in. It had neither an address nor a phone number. Early meetings convened in a Starbucks near a Metro stop in downtown Washington."[18]

Perhaps most importantly, while HAVA addressed the symptoms we saw in Florida 2000, it failed to address their root causes: the election system is usually underfunded, often run by people without adequate training, and occasionally hijacked to serve partisan ends. As long as Congress focuses on symptoms rather than root causes, it will be engaged in the policymaking equivalent of whack-a-mole.

Little wonder that serious problems persist. The same problems we saw in Florida—discarded ballots, improperly purged registration lists, poor ballot design—continue to rear their ugly heads. And a slew of new problems has emerged in HAVA's wake. For example, many jurisdictions used HAVA funds to purchase touch-screen machines that "are too easily compromised or hacked" and have an unacceptably high failure rate.[19] A group of computer scientists at Princeton conducted a security test on the country's most widely used electronic voting machines. They discovered that someone with one minute's access to the machine could upload a virus that would change vote totals without detection and, worse, spread the virus to other machines.[20]

We deserve better. Our democratic practices fall too short of our democratic ideals. Many describe voting as a civic sacrament. Paeans to the right to vote abound. People have put their lives on the line to exercise the right. And yet we neglect virtually every aspect of the process by which ballots are cast and counted. At a time when the United States is trying to spread democracy abroad, our election system falls well short of our peers'. We deserve a system that makes it easy for voters to register and cast a ballot. We deserve a system that counts votes accurately. We deserve a system that cannot be hijacked for political ends. We deserve a system that gives us the information we need to know how it's working. We deserve better.

THE CAUSE OF THE PROBLEM

It is bewildering that our system works as badly as the evidence suggests. After all, it's hard to find a more superficially appealing cause than democratic reform. How did we end up in this mess, and why can't we fix it?

Partisanship and localism—two features that distinguish our system from other developed democracies—are the main culprits. We leave the regulation of politics *to* politics; partisan officials administer large swaths of our election system. And ours is a highly decentralized system; we vest a tremendous amount of power in the hands of state and local officials. The combined effect of partisanship and localism undermines the quality of our election system and makes change hard to come by.

Foxes Guarding the Henhouse: The Problem of Partisanship

The United States is an outlier among mature democracies. Every other established democracy relies on professional administrators, insulated from political interference, to run its elections.[21] Here we depend on partisans.[22] The problem is so pervasive that academics routinely describe it as "foxes guarding the henhouse."[23]

Partisan bias. It's easy to see why it is a bad idea to have partisan officials run our elections. We don't let people referee the game they are playing, and with good reason. It creates too many opportunities for partisan mischief. The problem is not just that election officials are likely to root for their own political party. The problem is that election officials *depend on their party for their jobs.*

Consider the dilemma faced by an elected secretary of state, the most common overseer of elections in the United States. The position is widely thought to be a stepping stone for higher office. What matters most for the many secretaries of state who want to run for governor or Congress? Political support, not professional performance. When voters have little information about how well the election system is working, the fate of a secretary of state depends heavily on her standing within the party, which will provide resources and support for her next campaign. The current state of affairs creates the wrong kinds of incentives for secretaries of state—and the many partisan officials below them, whose careers similarly depend on partisan rather than professional credentials. As Chris Nelson, South Dakota's straight-shooting secretary of state, told me, "Being nonpartisan doesn't earn a lot of points with the party faithful."[24]

The most disturbing consequence of partisans administering our elections is political bias. Politics, after all, is a game devoted to helping your friends and hurting your enemies. It is possible to do both when administering elections. Most election policies have partisan consequences. Making it easier to vote is thought to help Democrats; making it harder to vote is thought to help Republicans. If you think that older people are likely to vote for your candidate, you will want to make it easier to vote absentee. Because people can be deterred by long lines, you will want to reduce the number of polling places or voting machines in areas where your opponent's supporters live.

Unsurprisingly, those with the motive and opportunity to engage in partisan shenanigans sometimes do the dirty deed. The authors of an important new study examining the election systems of five Midwestern states write that "it has been disconcerting to learn the extent to which the mindset of elected policymakers is not on how to design the voting process for the public's benefit, but rather on how to advance one's candidacy or party."[25] One of the authors of that study, Ohio State professor Dan Tokaji, terms efforts to hijack election rules to further partisan ends "the new vote denial."[26] The irony, of course, is that the "new vote denial" looks a lot like the old vote denial. We are back to worrying about the use of basic administrative practices to prevent citizens from voting. The new vote denial techniques may not work as directly as the strategies of Jim Crow. But politicians plainly think they are effective enough to use them.

Kenneth Blackwell, who served as Ohio's secretary of state during the 2004 presidential election, is a favorite target of complaint.[27] A Republican who was then chair of the Bush reelection campaign in Ohio, Blackwell publicly campaigned for President Bush and other conservative causes during his tenure. Blackwell was roundly criticized for administering the presidential election in a partisan fashion. Ohio was a battleground state, and both parties were fighting hard for every vote. The conventional wisdom was that high turnout would favor Kerry. Many thus suspected Blackwell's motives when he repeatedly made it more difficult to register and cast a ballot. For example, Blackwell ruled that voter registration cards had to be submitted on eighty-pound card stock, the heavy paper used for wedding invitations. It is difficult to imagine a sensible justification for such a rule, and easy to see how it could advance the Republicans' chances. Little wonder, then, that even members of Blackwell's own party were unwilling to stand by his decision, forcing him eventually to withdraw the regulation. Blackwell generated more controversy when he invoked his title in recording an automated telephone message urging voters to vote in favor of a constitutional amendment prohibiting same-sex unions.

Blackwell did little to improve his reputation during 2006, when he served as Ohio's chief elections officer at the same time that he ran for governor. Though Blackwell recused himself from ruling directly on a challenge to his opponent's eligibility, he made several decisions that were thought to improve the political fortunes of Republicans, including himself. For example, Blackwell interpreted Ohio's election code to require paid registration drive workers to return registration forms in person. The decision outraged get-out-the-vote groups and was ultimately enjoined by a state court. We will never know, of course, whether partisanship motivated Blackwell in making these decisions. At the very least, his actions created the appearance of political bias.

While most secretaries of state don't prompt such a ruckus, the perils of partisanship loom over them. In the words of Kentucky's dynamic young secretary of state, Trey Grayson, partisan affiliation puts election officers in a "potentially tough situation" if they plan to run for higher office.[28] Grayson argues that you "can't take the politics out" of these decision and you shouldn't "pretend there's not a problem."[29] Transparency, he insists, is the only solution.

The lack of professionalism. While bias is the most disturbing consequence of partisanship, it's not the most common. The vast majority of election administrators are people of good faith who do a very hard job with very few resources. But the problem of partisanship goes deeper than the biased administration of elections.

One unfortunate by-product of partisanship is a lack of professionalism. A system that depends on the political parties to staff it is unlikely to be staffed with trained experts. Just talk to Conny McCormack, L.A. County's former registrar-recorder. One of the most widely respected election administrators in the field, she exudes such competence that you sometimes wonder whether she'd be running IBM if her career path had taken a different turn.

McCormack is scathing about the role politics plays in election administration. She has run into enough tussles to recognize that some politicking is inevitable in the job. But the politicking goes too far, in her view, in states where secretaries of state are elected. McCormack argues that elected secretaries of state are not interested in "best practices or technical details." Those issues won't help them "get headlines and run for governor," she notes acidly. Top elections officials are largely focused on "raw partisan politics"; one succeeds by being a "charismatic campaigner, not a good administrator." The core problem, says McCormack, is that the skills necessary to run a campaign and the skills necessary to run an election system "don't necessarily match up."[30]

Though McCormack is too generous to admit it,[31] the lack of professionalism is a problem that runs through the system. Even at the local level, the overriding qualification for administering elections is often party membership, not professional qualifications. As a result, local election administrators are usually amateurs. They are people of good faith, but they lack the professional training or experience enjoyed by election administrators in other mature democracies. Moreover, like candidates for secretary of state, some harbor higher political ambitions. As a result, as election lawyer Bob Bauer observes, "Even the best-intentioned have other plans and commitments, priorities higher than the conduct of flawless elections, and a set of skills that do not necessarily include a deft touch for management."[32]

Resistance to change. Partisanship not only causes many of the problems in our election system, but makes it resistant to change. The obvious solution to the problem of partisanship is to replace politicians with bureaucrats whose jobs do not depend on their political standing. But when foxes are guarding the henhouse, it is hard to jettison them from that powerful station. The people who decide who decides—the federal and state legislators who have the power to place our election system in the hands of nonpartisans—are partisans themselves. And if you are the party in control, what incentive do you have to abandon this important weapon in your political arsenal? It's not a coincidence that election reform proposals tend to come from the party out of power, which loses interest in reform the moment it gains a majority of seats.

I once testified in favor of a nonpartisan districting in front of the Massachusetts state legislature. One bemused representative asked the question that I suspect was on the mind of many of his Democratic colleagues. Why, he asked, should Massachusetts Democrats "unilaterally disarm," giving up the power to draw districting plans that favored Democrats, without a guarantee that Texas Republicans would do the same? My job, of course, was to play the straight man to his cynical barb, so I blathered on about Massachusetts's leadership role in pushing progressive reform. The truth was that he had a point. It was not in the interests of Massachusetts Democrats to give up the power to district.

Politicians can even be reluctant to make changes that help their own party. Just ask Joe Mansky, who moved from a career in hydrology to become a highly respected elections official in Minnesota. Politicians, he says, "are reluctant to change the system that got them elected."[33] It's not hard to see the logic. If you granted politicians one wish for the next election, they'd all ask for the same thing: a voting pool that looks exactly like it did in the last election. You don't want anyone new from the other party to vote. And adding more members of your own party to the voter rolls might just invite a primary challenge.

Even when elections are administered by bipartisan boards, the parties have every reason to maintain the status quo. The one thing that Republicans and Democrats can generally agree upon is that the rules that got their incumbents elected should be kept in place. Moreover, local officials are reluctant to cede their jobs to nonpartisan boards. Those positions can be a political plum that the parties dole out to their most loyal supporters. It's the same problem McCormack sees in top offices: being a savvy politician is not the same thing as being a skilled administrator.

Local Competition and the Race to the Bottom

Localism is the other main source of the problems we see in election administration. While most mature democracies use a national bureaucracy to administer elections, the American system is highly decentralized. States run all of our elections, and most vest considerable authority in localities to carry out basic tasks like registering voters and counting ballots.

Decentralization is often a very good idea. It can encourage experimentation and policies tailored to local needs. In the elections context, however, decentralization has caused so many problems that scholars condemn it as "hyper-decentralization"[34] or "failed federalism."[35]

The crux of the problem is that many election jurisdictions in the United States are starved for resources. Half the jurisdictions in the United States have fewer than 1,400 voters; two-thirds have fewer than 10,000 voters.[36] Small jurisdictions like these simply cannot hire enough people to staff elections. Most make due by having their election superintendents work part-time or perform multiple roles. These folks barely have time to carry out basic duties, let alone do the things we'd ideally want them to do.

If you want to know how hard the job is, just talk to Joy Streater, the county clerk for Comal County in Texas.[37] I was recently at a conference on collecting election data. A number of high-powered academics and big players in election administration flagged the challenges involved in collecting the information. No one was more effective than Streater. Her secret? She just described, in a low-key Texas drawl, what her average day looked like. It was fun to watch optimistic calls for change neatly deflated by Streater's aw-shucks-I'm-just-a-simple-country-clerk speech.

Think you have a hard job? Imagine your office had to register births and deaths; issue marriage licenses; record official public records; and record subdivisions plats, modifications, and amendments. Imagine you served as the clerk of the Commissioners Court and the County Court, the records management officer for all county offices processing all mental commitments, and a member of the Bail Bond Board, the Reclassification Committee, and some strange institution called the Wellness Committee. And, by the way, you are also supposed to run all local, state, and federal elections. If you are Joy Streater, you'll also win a bunch of awards, testify regularly before the state legislature, and serve on various advisory boards.

Streater is quick to remind you that she's actually better off than most county clerks. Comal County is a fairly large jurisdiction by Texas standards. She has only one part-time person running elections, but at least that person has 34 years of experience and has been able to make due with the temporary help they hire around election time. But resources are still tight. When I spoke with Streater last June, she'd just come back from a meeting to plan for the general election. The problem on her mind? People wanted the county to keep all the early voting sites open for two weeks prior to the election. Sounds pretty reasonable, doesn't it?

"How much would it cost?" I asked her.

"One hundred thousand dollars," she said calmly.

"What is your overall budget?" I queried.

"We've got $125,000," she responded in honeyed tones, "so we'd have $25,000 left for everything else."

Reformers and academics have a bad tendency to genuflect toward the problem of local resources and then blithely go ahead and demand more from election administrators. I've done it more often than I care to admit. Talking to Joy Streater provides a bracing reminder of the challenges decentralization poses for those interested in reform.

Since you probably won't have a chance to watch Streater in action, let me give you some hard numbers on the resource challenges local officials face. The best study available was done by Eric Fischer, a senior specialist at the Congressional Research Service, along with his fellow CRS analyst Kevin Coleman.[38] With his bushy hair, booming voice, and amusing stories about John Bolton's adolescence (Bolton's dislike of the United Nations apparently dates back to seventh grade), Fischer seems like the last person you'd imagine studying a topic as dry as election administration. He is, after all, a man who has been attacked by Costa Rican peccaries and can talk for hours about the sex life of hermaphroditic sharks. But in the wake of the 2000 election, CRS needed someone to develop expertise in the field, and Fischer was happy to step up.

Fischer's national survey revealed that the average election official doesn't possess a college degree and earns less than $50,000 per year, with some local officials earning as little as $10,000 per year.[39] The average local official oversees a wide range of responsibilities beyond running elections but has received fewer than twenty hours of training.[40] Most local officials are worried about future funding.[41]

If you want a more granular view of the resource issue, you should talk to Gary Smith,[42] a man who could not be more different from Fischer. Smith, the director of elections in Forsyth County, Georgia, is a businessman's businessman. He speaks in a low-key but commanding style, and it's hard to imagine that a hermaphroditic fish would dare cross his path. Smith became the director of elections after retiring from a high-powered position in the private sector, where he oversaw international operations for a company with 250,000 employees. At the time, he thought election administration would be nice way to ease into retirement.

Smith conducted a comprehensive wage and benefits survey[43] of Georgia's election system for a simple reason.

"You get what you pay for," he says. When Smith first saw what his own salary would be, he assumed it was a part-time job. As he learned, "The only thing part-time about this job is the salary." Coming from the private sector, Smith had thought that applying private sector practices to government would quickly improve the system. "I didn't realize all of the constraints that people in the public sector have to deal with," he observes wryly. "It is *a lot* different." Imagine moving from a top corporate office to a place where staffers address envelopes by hand. Smith was thus acutely aware of the need for resources in election administration.

Smith approached the resource question just as any sensible businessperson would. He gathered data to assess whether there was a problem, something he's done for every job he's had. "It's like taking a snapshot," he notes. The results of his survey are stunning. Most registrars in Georgia make less than ten dollars an hour, with some getting paid roughly the minimum wage. Almost half of the survey respondents aren't covered by a retirement plan, the vast majority receive neither overtime nor comp time, and 79 percent report that they cannot expand their staff to keep up with their expanding workload. About half of the counties cannot afford to hire an elections superintendent, so the work gets done by probate judges, who are also poorly paid. Smith estimates that 80 percent of election administrators in Georgia don't possess a college degree. As with many states, Georgia's large jurisdictions have more staff and more resources. The problem, as Smith points out, is that while large counties may have more votes to process, the technical and legal responsibilities for small and large counties are the same. Failed federalism, indeed.

If you believe that you get what you pay for, it's a wonder that there are any Joy Streaters or Gary Smiths running our elections. Doug Chapin of electionline.org calls election administrators "grenade catchers,"[44] and rightly so. They deal with one potential crisis after another. They do a very hard job with remarkably few resources. And they are paid very little for performing a thankless task. When things go well, nobody notices. When things go badly, guess who ends up getting blamed?

Resistance to Change

As with partisanship, localism doesn't just undermine the quality of our system; it makes it hard to put a better one in place. When partisanship blocks change, it is because politics are working badly; representatives are putting their own interests ahead of their constituents'. But even when politics are working correctly—when politicians are attentive to what voters want—political incentives run the wrong way in election reform. That is because the costs of deferred maintenance are mostly invisible to voters. When a problem is invisible, local competition gives politicians every reason to neglect it.

The Problem of Invisibility

While problems in our voting system occur regularly, voters become aware of them only when an election is so close that they affect the outcome. Because such crises occur episodically, voters have a haphazard sense of how well our elections are run and no comparative data to tell them which systems work and which don't. The result is a failure of the political market.

In a federal system like our own, the invisibility of election problems reduces the incentives for even reform-minded politicians to invest in the system. One reason to favor decentralization is that states and localities will compete to win the hearts and minds of citizens, leading them to try to outdo each other in providing useful services and passing good policies. But states and localities will compete only along the dimensions that voters can see. When election problems are invisible, localities will invest in projects that voters can readily observe—roads, new schools, more cops on the beat. Just ask Matt Damschroder, former chair of the Franklin County Board of Elections in Ohio. "People don't view funding elections as a priority," he notes. They "throw resources" at reform only "after a crisis."[45]

Here again, academics use shorthand to describe this problem: "the race to the bottom."[46] We want local competition to create a virtuous race to the top, but sometimes it leads in the opposite direction. In a world where election problems are hard to detect, any jurisdiction that spends a lot on the election system is likely to be handicapped in competing for hearts and minds because it is diverting money from the visible to the invisible. In this respect, our failure to maintain our election infrastructure is quite similar to our failure to maintain our physical infrastructure. Both occur because voters see only the occasional and haphazardly distributed results of neglect but have no means to gauge how things are working generally. Deferred maintenance is a consequence of localism.

Problems compounded. The problems of localism compound the perils of partisanship in our election system. The partisan officials and amateurs who run the system do so with too little money and too few staff. It is hard for local administrators to perform basic election functions, let alone spend time on activities that would improve the system, like collecting performance data or studying best practices.

If the problem of invisibility weren't enough, partisanship makes it even harder for election officials to lobby for much-needed resources. Because politicians would much prefer to fund projects that are visible to voters, they are unlikely to be happy if a secretary of state or local administrator from their own party raises a ruckus about inadequate funding. It's the rough equivalent of airing the party's dirty laundry in public. As Secretary of State Grayson notes in his gentle southern drawl, "Calling them on it can make your friends mad."[47] If your job depends on your standing within the party, the incentives to stay quiet are significant.

It's not just your friends, though. As Grayson points out, things don't get any easier for the elections official seeking funding from members of the opposing party. While that official will feel comfortable drawing attention to funding shortfalls—he might even do so for partisan gain—the opposing party won't want to fix the problem. After all, why would a politician do anything that might promote the success of someone from the other party, especially someone who is likely to run for higher office in the future?[48] Ohio's secretary of state, Jennifer Brunner, told me that the same problem plays out at the local level.[49] In Ohio, for instance, a Democratic director of the local board of elections might be seeking resources from a county commission with a Republican majority, or vice versa.

Even when reform isn't costly, the tide of local competition runs against change. The financial capital of states and localities is limited, but so is their political capital. There are only so many issues that can make it on the agenda of top-level policymakers. Governors, legislators, even secretaries of state must pick and choose what issues will occupy their time. If voters don't pay much attention to a question, the odds are that state and local officials won't either.

Localism also makes it harder to create professional norms that would push election officials to do better. It's not just that local administrators barely have the time and resources to do their jobs, let alone travel to conferences or study up on best practices. Localism means that professional associations are organized at the state level, thus preventing the cross-state interactions that help good ideas spread.

Partisanship and localism combine to create a system that is deeply flawed and resistant to change. When politics work badly, partisanship taints the way elections are administered and makes the foxes reluctant to give up guarding the henhouse. When politics work well, states and localities compete to fund projects that voters can see, and neglect problems that voters can't. In both cases, our election system suffers. The perils of partisanship and the problems of localism explain why a cause as appealing as election reform has yet to take root.

THE SOLUTION
A Democracy Index

A Democracy Index represents a promising here-to-there strategy for redirecting the political incentives that run against reform. As I explain in detail in the next two chapters, we have shockingly little data on how our system is working, a problem that handicaps reform efforts from start to finish. By presenting the right information in the right form, a Democracy Index has the potential to harness partisanship and local competition in the service of reform. Indeed, at every stage of the reform process—from figuring out what reform is needed to getting change passed—the Democracy Index should help smooth the path for change.

What Should a Democracy Index Look Like? An Initial Take

Before making the case for a Democracy Index, it seems useful to explain what an Index would look like. Here I'll outline basic criteria for creating the Index and a brief explanation for why I chose them, leaving a discussion of methodological challenges and specific metrics for chapter 5. The analysis comes with some caveats.

First, this sketch is an opening gambit in a long-term conversation. Academics sometimes bear an uncomfortable resemblance to Henry Luce, about whom it was said, "Sometimes right, sometimes wrong, never in doubt." It would be foolish to have a firm view on how the Index should be designed at this early stage of the process. The Index must appeal to a wide range of stakeholders—voters, experts, election administrators, policymakers, and reformers. Their input will necessarily and quite properly give shape to the Index. Moreover, any effort to create a Democracy Index will involve a "pushmi-pullyu" process. Whether designers of the Index begin with the ideal or the real, they will have to toggle back and forth between what we want to measure and what we can measure.

Second, what I sketch below is an ideal. As the next chapter makes clear, we don't yet have the data we need to build the Index I describe here. I'll have a lot more to say about collecting the data in chapter 5. For now, I'll just describe what we should be shooting for.

Finally, in order to avoid getting bogged down in too many details this early in the game, I offer more detailed justifications and responses to counterarguments in the endnotes. If you flip to them, you'll see something that would look excessive to anyone but a law professor.

A Nuts-and-Bolts Approach

What should the Democracy Index measure? Should it focus on nuts-and-bolts issues (the basic mechanics of election administration) or the broader democratic health of the polity (something that would look to campaign finance laws, the quality of public debate, and civil-rights issues)? I strongly flavor a nuts-and-bolts approach. If the Index is going to help get us from here to there, it must get political traction. Designers of the Index should therefore be risk averse in the way politicians are risk averse, avoiding metrics that could create enough controversy to sink the entire endeavor. That means focusing on the lived experience of the average voter while eschewing hot-button topics like felon disenfranchisement or campaign finance. Public opinion matters, especially in choosing the basic measurement categories. But we should also leave room for technical issues that appear on the radar screens of experts but not voters. The goal here is simply to identify commonsense criteria on which a large number of people could agree if those criteria were explained.

The Democracy Index should also focus on issues squarely within election administrators' control rather than punish them for problems that exceed their grasp. For example, some problems in the election system are outside an administrator's control. Low turnout, for instance, is caused in part by socioeconomics and the absence of competitive elections. Administrators in low-ranked states will not bother with a ranking that expects them to remedy systemic problems associated with poverty or compensate for a lack of excitement about a race. If you are going to look to turnout to assess how well the system is working, you'll have to be able to disentangle the problems within an election administrator's control (like making it hard to register or to cast a ballot) and those outside of it. The key is to differentiate between "luck and skill," as political scientist Thad Hall puts it.[50]

Three Simple Things

These two criteria—what should matter to the average voter? what is fairly within the ambit of an election administrator's control?—suggest that the Index ought to focus on three simple things: (1) registering voters, (2) casting ballots, and (3) counting votes.* These represent simple, intuitive categories built around the experiences of voters, and they mirror the cyclical rhythms of the administrator's job.

Measure Performance

The next question, of course, is *how* to measure these three simple things. We could assess election systems based on the quality of their policy "inputs." How good is the registration system? Does the jurisdiction train its poll workers properly? Are ballots counted using best practices? Alternatively, we could assess the system based on performance "outputs." How many errors are in the registration lists? How long were the lines? How many ballots got discarded?[51]

I strongly favor assessing election systems based on performance outputs whenever the data can be had. At the end of the day, voters and top-level policymakers—two key audiences for the Index—don't care what policies a jurisdiction chooses; they care about the *results* of those choices. Moreover, because we don't yet have good comparative data on performance outputs, it's not clear that we really know what constitutes good policy and what doesn't. Finally, performance data are considerably easier to use for making comparisons. Those data are not yet standardized, but they can be. Comparing policy inputs against one another, in contrast, is tough. It's hard to envision a benchmark other than a gut-level instinct that something is "better." For example, it should be easier to compare the number of complaints from poll workers that a jurisdiction receives than to decide whether the best way to train poll workers is through an online system, an in-person lecture, or a hands-on demonstration. It will be easier to com-

*Needless to say, the architects of the Index should answer these questions based on focus group research and polling. Though I haven't had a fleet of polls to inform my views, I have had the good fortune to receive a number of thoughtful comments from social scientists, law professors, and election administrators.

pare the number of people who try to register but fail than to make an atmospheric assessment of whether the registration system is a good one.

If we cast our three simple categories in performance terms, the Index should assess how close a jurisdiction comes to reaching these goals:

Every eligible voter who wants to register can do so.

Every registered voter who wants to cast a ballot can do so.

Every ballot cast is counted properly.

Hard Data over Subjective Assessments

In measuring performance, the Index should rely on hard data over subjective assessments wherever possible. Quantitative data will be more convincing to voters and policymakers than atmospheric assessments. And quantitative data offer a more sensible baseline for comparing election performance across jurisdictions.*

Balancing Values: Convenience, Integrity, and Accuracy

Note that our three simple performance categories encompass the two major values invoked in any election debate: *convenience* and *integrity.*[52] When reform debates take place, liberals typically emphasize the importance of convenience—making it easier to register or cast a ballot—whereas conservatives tend to talk about integrity, by which they mean preventing

*Just to give a concrete sense of what these categories (policy inputs / performance outputs, quantitative data / qualitative assessments) mean in practice, consider a simple measurement question. Suppose you decided that the length of lines at polling places was something the Index ought to measure. The following options would be available to you:

Data	*Policy inputs*	*Performance outputs*
Qualitative	Were poll workers well trained? Was the preelection planning done well?	Did voters think they spent too long in line?
Quantitative	How many machines were allocated per voter? How many poll workers were allocated per voter?	How long did voters spend in line?

fraud. It's the electoral equivalent of the "tastes great / less filling" debate, and just about as illuminating. Any outsider to this debate would think that we are required to make some existential choice—convenience or integrity, making it easier to vote or preventing fraud—in creating an election system. But both values matter, and the best we can do is make sensible trade-offs between them.

There is a third value that is rarely mentioned in partisan fights, presumably because everyone believes in it: *accuracy*. People on both sides of the partisan divide believe that registration information should be transferred accurately onto the voter roll, that ballots should correctly register the preference of the person who cast it, and that the vote count should precisely reflect the ballots cast.

When we think of these three values—convenience, integrity, and accuracy—it's clear that each becomes more or less salient depending on the stage of the process. At the registration stage, all three values matter. Voters want it to be easy to register. They want the state to record their information accurately on the voter roll. And they don't want ineligible people to be registered. At the balloting stage, in contrast, voters care mostly about convenience and accuracy. They want polling places that are easy to find, poll workers who are helpful, and balloting machines that are easy to use. And they also want the ballot they cast to reflect their preferences correctly. Finally, at the counting stage, integrity and accuracy are crucial. Voters want the ballots cast to be counted accurately, and they want election results untainted by fraud. Folding the values convenience, integrity, and accuracy into the process categories I have proposed helps us focus on the right value at the right time. The following table captures the basic values the Index should emphasize at each stage of the process:

	Registration	*Balloting*	*Counting*
Performance goal	Every eligible voter who wants to register can do so.	Every registered voter who wants to cast a ballot can do so.	Every ballot cast is counted properly.
Relevant values	Convenience, integrity, and accuracy	Convenience and accuracy	Integrity and accuracy

Simple Categories, Reasonably Comprehensive Metrics

Albert Einstein once said that things should be as simple as possible, but no simpler, a useful aphorism for designing the Index. Because the basic performance categories that structure the Index are its "public face,"[53] they should be as simple and intuitive as possible. These categories "receive[ ] the vast majority of the attention" from the public and policymakers,[54] says David Roodman, chief architect of the Commitment to Development Index. "Top level accessibility is invaluable," he continues, because "a reader who can easily understand the ideal and overall structure of an Index will feel oriented and more prepared to buy into the whole construct."[55] It is for precisely this reason that I've suggested organizing the data around three intuitive categories that capture the most important aspects of the election process from both the voter's and administrator's perspective.

As one moves from top-level categories to individual metrics, however, the Index's architects should use reasonably comprehensive metrics within each category. I am not suggesting comprehensiveness for its own sake. The closer a single metric gets to measuring what we want to measure, the fewer metrics the Index will need. Think, for instance, about the elegant simplicity of the residual vote rate, a measurement that political scientists at the Caltech/MIT Voting Technology Project invented in the wake of the 2000 election.[56] The residual vote rate measures the difference "between the number of voters appearing on Election Day and the number of ballots actually counted."[57]

We wouldn't expect the residual vote rate to be zero; even in a well-run system, some voters cast a ballot without voting for anyone for president. But it makes an excellent comparative measure. That's because we'd expect the number of people who don't vote for a presidential candidate to be roughly constant. If a jurisdiction's residual vote rate is higher than average, it's a good bet that the number is caused by problems we would expect election officials to correct—poor machines, bad ballot design, or tabulation errors. Moreover, the residual vote rate is a pure performance measure that captures something that really matters to voters—whether their ballots got counted.

If we could come up with rough equivalent of a residual vote rate for each of the three categories noted above, we'd be most of the way to constructing an Index. But at least early on, we won't have data sets that perfectly capture what we want to measure. We'll thus have to rely on imperfect substitutes. Redundancy can serve a useful purpose in this context. It can help us gauge whether the proxies we have chosen are working (because we can see whether metrics rise and fall together), discourage jurisdictions from diverting resources just to improve their scores (because it will be harder to focus on improving one or two measurements while neglecting their other duties), and provide a backstop against cheating (because we can see if self-reported data are radically different from data obtained elsewhere).[58]

Proxies and Pragmatism

The guidelines above tell us what the Democracy Index would look like in the ideal. It's an attainable ideal, but an ideal nonetheless. The question is what we should do in the meantime.

At a minimum, early versions of the Index will have to rely on proxies to measure election performance. Sometimes that means using subjective measures or policy inputs. Sometimes we will have to measure pieces of the problem because we cannot assess the whole. Sometimes the data will be so flawed that we'll have to drop a metric until better data are found.

As designers of other indices will attest, pragmatism is the key. "Don't let the perfect be the enemy of the good" is a trite, worn-out, pedestrian phrase that ought to be confined to the dustbin of literary history. But there's a reason for that. Whenever I have spoken with someone who'd assembled an index, he or she has emphasized the need to use reasonable proxies to measure what you want to measure (in a transparent fashion, of course). An imperfect prototype is one of the best tools for pushing data collection forward. It not only publicizes gaps in the data, but lays down a template for what information should be collected going forward.

Consider, for instance, what happened in the wake of the creation of the Quality Counts schools assessment. When the first report was released, only a handful of school systems collected the information Quality Counts wanted. By creating a necessarily imperfect but nonetheless useful first report, Quality Counts laid down a marker for what information a school ought to collect if it is "serious about performance," says Lynn Olson. Over time, that marker has prompted many school systems to collect precisely the information that the first version of Quality Counts had identified as important.[59]

Let me give you a quick example of the way proxies could work for the Democracy Index. In chapter 5, I'll suggest that a reasonably comprehensive, performance-based measure for assessing the registration process would be how many eligible voters who tried to register were able to do so successfully. That's hard to measure right now. So what proxies might we use to get a read on how well the registration process is working? We might try to identify the reasons why registration systems fail and assess them seriatim. For instance, one reason that people might be deterred from registering is because it's too hard. So we might use testers to figure out how easy it is for people to register to vote. Or rely on what I call "Nielsen voters"—randomly chosen voters who would record their experience with the voting process—to give us a rough sense of how easy it is to register. Or randomly tag some fraction of the registration cards being filed and follow those cards through the process.[60] Similarly, another reason that people who try to register might fail is that election administrators enter the information into the system incorrectly. One way to get a rough sense of how well the data-entry process is working is to count the number of empty "fields" in the state's registration database or compare the state's registration list against the database of a mail solicitation or credit card company, which have compiled extremely accurate databases. These kinds of metrics should serve as good proxies for what we are really trying to assess.

Weight Scores in the Top-level Categories in a Simple, Transparent Fashion

Once the metrics in each category have been assembled, you'll have to aggregate them into an Index. Scores in the top-level categories—registration, balloting, and counting—should be weighted equally, just as one calculates a grade point average. This weighting strategy is highly intuitive, and there is no obvious principle that would dictate a different strategy At least until we have more information about what how voters and policymakers think about these questions, it makes sense to go with the simplest, most transparent strategy. I'll say more about the weighting question in chapter 4. For now, I'll just note that the method I propose here comports with the experiences of the creators of other indices.[61]

Within Categories, Weight Based on What's Available

Although we should use a simple weighting strategy when adding the broad categories of the Index together, we can't do that with individual metrics. Here the costs of simplicity are too great. For instance, imagine that we came up with twenty-five different ways to measure the length of lines but only one reasonable metric for assessing the service provided by poll workers. It's hard to imagine using a twenty-five-to-one ratio for weighting the two categories. Or imagine that fifty thousand people ended up waiting in line for more than an hour in both Rhode Island and California. Needless to say, it wouldn't be fair to compare those numbers given the population disparities between the states. You also can't just add numbers together across categories. Imagine that fifty thousand people stood in long lines it Rhode Island, and fifty-three of its polling places opened late. No one would think that adding those two numbers together would produce a meaningful measure. As these examples suggest, some statistical work will be necessary to convert raw data into standardized metrics that can be sensibly compared.[62]

Rank, Don't Grade

If the data are good enough, the Index should rank, not grade—aggregating the data into a single, composite ranking (e.g., rank the states 1–50). There are alternatives, of course. The Index might rank jurisdictions within categories but provide no composite ranking. Or it could award jurisdictions one or more letter grades. Assuming the data are good enough, ranking is the best option. Rankings get more political traction than the alternatives, precisely because they reduce the data to their simplest form.[63]

Rank Localities

If the data are good enough, the Index should rank not just states, but localities. In many places, local jurisdictions are where the action is. Moreover, ranking localities helps protect state officials from being punished when the state's ranking falls because of the poor performance of a few local outliers. Given the amount of variation within states, ranking localities would also help us identify best practices and the drivers of performance.

Be Transparent

No matter how the Index is designed, the choices made—and the reasons behind them—should be as transparent as possible. Not only should the designers of the Index explain each category and metric, but they should describe how the data were aggregated and explain how different choices might have affected the results. The layout of the Index's website and report should mirror the structure of the Index itself, with simple explanations provided at the front and more detailed, technical information available to anyone who wants to drill down into the details.[64] And all of the data and calculations should be posted for review and critique.

Offer One-stop Shopping

Although the Index should rank states and localities based on performance outputs, it should not ignore policy inputs. To the contrary, our best hope for identifying best practices and the drivers of performance is to know which policies led to which results. Ideally, the Index should give election officials the policymaking equivalent of one-stop shopping. Imagine, for instance, you were an election official unhappy with your score. The Index would be most useful if you could identify the categories where your state underperformed and figure out what states did well. The website would describe the policies that led to high scores and link to information and resources that would help you implement a similar policy.

Adapt, Adapt, Adapt

Needless to say, the Index should change over time. It will take time to develop the right kind of data. It will take time to work out the kinks in the design. It will take time to spot problems and remedy them. Moreover, there is likely to be a natural growth cycle for the Index. At the beginning, the dearth of data will narrow the Index's focus. If and when the Index catches on, we'll have to deal with different problems, like states gaming the numbers. The key is to imagine each version of the Democracy Index as a step in the conversation, not a final answer.

None of this should discourage us from trying. It always takes time to develop a good index. The gross domestic product—among the most respected and useful indices ever developed—has taken more than 70 years to perfect. Every decade since its inception, changes in economic conditions and advances in economic theory have resulted in significant modifications to the measure. Similarly, each of the indices discussed in this book has been retooled as its creators learned from past mistakes. If anyone has managed to design an index correctly the first time, he is either a mad genius or should head to Vegas before his luck runs out.

CONCLUSION

The perverse politics of election reform are well known in election circles. But phrases like "the foxes guarding the henhouse" or "the race to the bottom" are typically conclusions to an argument, not a starting point for further inquiry. Academics and reformers often argue that elections should be administered by a centralized bureaucracy fully insulated from politics. But a nonpartisan, centralized system for administering elections does not spring, as did Athena, fully formed from the head of a god. It has to be created by somebody, usually an elected somebody, and that is where the here-to-there question kicks in. Those in power have every incentive to maintain the status quo. Reformers thus spend a good deal of time asking politicians and local officials to do something contrary to their self-interest. Perhaps unsurprisingly, that strategy has not yielded terribly impressive results.

Rather than focusing on proposals that require the foxes to stop guarding the henhouse or imagining that our centuries-old tradition of localism will vanish overnight, we should think more about how to domesticate the foxes and harness the power of local competition. While this type of here-to-there strategy may not seem as grand as an overhaul of the system, it offers a more realistic hope of effecting change in the long run. We do not have an ideal system in place. But we might as well take advantage of the best features of the current system—the powerful engine of partisanship and the intriguing possibilities associated with local competition—to create an environment in which bigger and better reform is possible.

A Democracy Index is promising strategy for getting from here to there because it puts the right information into the right form. An Index would measure the basic things that matter to voters: registering, balloting, and counting. Whenever possible, it would emphasize hard data and bottom-line results. And the Index would weight the data in a simple, intuitive fashion in order to rank states and localities based on their performance. There are devils in those details, as I discuss in chapters 4 and 5. But for now, this should suffice as a rough blueprint for the Index. In the next two chapters, I'll explain why putting the right information in the right form can help reverse the political tides that have so long run against reform.

2 The Promise of Data-driven Reform

As chapter 1 makes clear, partisanship and localism generate political tides that run against election reform. If we want to get from "here to there," we need a solution that will redirect those tides. Ranking states and localities based on performance can do just that. At every stage of the process, a Democracy Index should help smooth the path for change.

This chapter tells a tale of two reformers. The first is Spencer Overton, an election reformer who fights the good fight in a world without data. The second is Dan Esty, who has used data-driven performance rankings to change the way we talk about environmental policy. The chapter closes by explaining why the Democracy Index should help us chose intelligent solutions for the problems that face us, leaving for the next chapter a discussion of how the Index can help get those solutions passed.

A TALE OF TWO REFORMERS

A New-style Reformer Encounters an Old Problem

Spencer Overton, professor of law at George Washington University, doesn't fit the stereotype of an election reformer.[1] Polished and professional, it's easier to imagine him in Armani than Birkenstocks. Overton draws his idealism from a civil-rights background, and he is capable of talking about the right to vote in stirring terms. But with his Harvard Law degree and measured baritone, it's as easy to imagine him relating to corporate executives as to public interest lawyers. Perhaps unsurprisingly, Overton has often served as a translator for the reform community. His first book recast complex and sometimes arcane election law questions in terms that everyone can understand.[2] In Overton's words, the goal of the book is to show "the relationship between the technical details of election administration and big questions of power."[3]

People have written a good deal about the new generation of reformers. Entrepreneurial and pragmatic, they eschew old political divides and attack problems with the hard head of a corporate executive. They look to a variety of institutions (the market, administrative agencies), not just the courts, for solutions. They are as likely to appeal to business-minded ideas—accountability, competition—as progressive values like participation and empowerment. Overton perfectly embodies this new style.

Overton's problem is that he is fighting for change in a world without data. Indeed, he found himself in the middle of one of the biggest election reform battles we've seen in recent years—one that made it all the way to the Supreme Court—and lost in large part because he didn't have the data he needed to make his case.

The fight was over voter identification—the requirement that voters show a government-issued photo ID when they cast a ballot at the polls. Voter ID has been a significant source of contention in election circles. Conservative commentators insist that an ID requirement deters fraud. Liberal commentators counter that the requirement is a disguised effort to suppress (largely Democratic) votes.* The rhetoric on both sides of the issue has been quite heated, with one side talking about stolen elections and the other side equating ID requirements with vote suppression.

Overton became embroiled in the issue when it was taken up by the Commission on Federal Election Reform, chaired by former Democratic president Jimmy Carter and former Republican secretary of state James Baker. Though most of the members of the bipartisan commission had strong political ties, it included a handful of academics, including Overton.

The Carter-Baker Commission eventually staked out a position on voter ID that looked an awful lot like a political deal.[4] It roughly tracked the compromise that would emerge if a prominent Democrat and a prominent

*That's because many people from traditionally Democratic constituencies—poor people, racial minorities—lack a driver's license and would find it cumbersome to get an ID.

Republican sat down to work out something both sides could live with. The commission blessed the ID requirement (something Republicans usually want) while demanding that the state take affirmative steps to distribute IDs (something that Democrats would want if forced to accept an ID requirement).

Deal or no deal, the main problem with the commission's position was that it was utterly unsupported by empirical evidence. A pure political compromise can be produced without coming to grips with the empirics; a sound decision cannot. Although the commission did an excellent job of amassing data on how our election system is run in many areas, this was not one where it managed to find much. As the commission itself stated, there is "no extensive evidence of fraud in the United States."[5] To the extent there is any evidence of fraud, it is almost entirely due to absentee voting scams or ballot-box stuffing, not the type of fraudulent in-person voting that photo ID is supposed to deter. The only other justification that the commission offered for its decision was that a photo ID requirement would enhance public trust in the system. That claim, too, was unsupported by empirical evidence (and may have been misplaced).[6]

Overton did his best to persuade the other members of the commission not to endorse an ID requirement. Most advocates contesting voter ID have simply invoked civil-rights rhetoric. Overton called upon that tradition, but he mainly focused on the kind of cold-blooded cost-benefit arguments that conservatives stereotypically use. Working with the Brennan Center, he tried to amass data on the effects, good and bad, of photo ID. When he failed to change the majority's mind, he published a forcefully worded dissent. I saw Overton a day after the fight went public. I've never seen anyone more exhausted.

The reason Overton faced such an uphill slog is that the data were haphazard and inconsistent. As he discovered, "No systematic, empirical study of the magnitude of voter fraud has been conducted at either the national level or in any state to date."[7] Nor were there any good studies on an ID requirement's effect on voter behavior. Overton pulled together some basic numbers (how many voters lack ID, how many fraudulent votes might have been prevented by an ID requirement). Based on these numbers, he argued that it would be a mistake to endorse voter ID at this stage because the commission could not show that it "would exclude even one fraudulent vote for every 1000 eligible voters excluded."[8] But Overton candidly admitted that his data, standing alone, could not tell you what would happen if an ID requirement were enacted.[9]

Overton and the Carter-Baker Commission as a whole had the same problem: they were fighting about reform in a world without data. The Carter-Baker Commission justified its conclusions with the only evidence available: anecdote. Overton believed that anecdotal evidence led the commission to overestimate both the problem of fraud and the likelihood that an ID requirement would solve it.[10] Overton did not spare his allies criticism, either. He rebuked opponents of voter ID because they "regularly recite talking points about threats to voter participation by the poor and minorities, but often fail to quantify this assertion."[11] Overton's frustration about the debate remains palpable: "I'm an academic," he says. "I believe in facts."[12]

The same year that the Carter-Baker Commission released its report, the Republican-dominated Indiana legislature passed a photo ID requirement in a straight party-line vote. The state conceded it was not aware of a single episode of in-person voter fraud in its entire history, and the legislature failed to do anything about the security of absentee ballots (the one area where Indiana had recently had a fraud problem). "Let's not beat around the bush," wrote one of the lower-court judges reviewing the case. "The Indiana voter photo ID law is a not-too-thinly-veiled attempt to discourage election-day turnout by certain folks believed to skew Democratic."[13]

When the lawsuit challenging Indiana's law worked its way to the Supreme Court, Justice Stevens, writing for the plurality, upheld the requirement.[14] He concluded that photo ID was a reasonable strategy for combating fraud and building voter confidence. What evidence did Justice Stevens cite in support? A funny anecdote dating back to Tammany Hall, the fact that one person had voted fraudulently in a Washington gubernatorial election . . . and the Carter-Baker Report.

The problem is obvious. The Supreme Court didn't have much evidence to cite for its view that in-person vote fraud was a problem. So it cited the Carter-Baker Report, which in turn didn't have much evidence to cite. The Supreme Court had no evidence to cite for its intuition that an ID requirement boosts voter confidence. So it cited the Carter-Baker Commission, which in turn had no evidence to cite. It's turtles all the way down.

The Bigger Story

The debate over voter ID is part of a larger story about reform in a world without data. The story has an obvious moral—whether your intuitions are closer to Justice Stevens's or Spencer Overton's, surely you'd prefer the decision rested on data. But it also gives you a flavor for what reform debates look like in a world without data.

Note, for instance, what kind of reform proposals get traction in a world without data. Most reforms never see the light of day, as I discussed in the last chapter. The rare proposals that do get traction are those with intuitive appeal, like an ID requirement. Middle-class voters are accustomed to showing ID to get on a plane or pay with a credit card, so it's easy to frame the issue in a way that they can understand. (Think about the only other issue to get traction in recent years—paper trails for voting machines. It's another issue people can wrap their hands around.) There's no reason, of course, to think that intuitively appealing reform is the right reform. But the best strategy for defeat mistaken intuitions—testing them empirically—is impossible in a world without data.

Worse, in the absence of data, reform debates are completely at the mercy of politics. The reason photo ID got passed in Indiana is because it aligned with partisan incentives and the other side couldn't build a case against it. (Lest you think I'm picking on the Republicans, I should emphasize that Democrats are similarly inclined to oppose photo ID because of their own political interests. Remember, the Indiana law was passed without a single Democratic defector.) Similarly, when the Carter-Baker Commission announced its position on voter ID, it had no empirical basis to think it was announcing good policy. All that the Carter-Baker Commission could offer was a position that both political parties could live with. Here again, there is no reason to think that "change the parties can live with" bears any resemblance to the change we need.

Just think about how hard it is to referee this fight. There are lots of accusations and few facts. The Republicans and Democrats shout about partisanship. Reformers hint darkly about voter suppression. Whether you are a voter or a Supreme Court justice, it's hard to figure out who is right unless you subscribe to Lev Tolstoy's wry claim that "among coachmen, as among us all, whoever starts shouting at others with the greatest self-assurance, and shouts first, is right."[15]

Finally, and most importantly, note that the ultimate referees of this fight—members of the Supreme Court—were hungry for guidance. The Court encountered the dilemma we all face in the elections context: distinguishing between legitimate efforts to regulate the election system and illicit attempts to hijack it for political ends. The justices were plainly on the hunt for a yardstick to evaluate the Indiana law. Justice Stevens wasn't the only one to rely on the Carter-Baker Report. The dissenting justices did so as well. Unfortunately, it wasn't a very good yardstick for the justices to use. The Carter-Baker Commission had nothing to go on except atmospherics and anecdote. All it could offer is a compromise that smelled like a political deal. The voter ID fight makes clear just how powerful a yardstick can be in election debates. Even an imperfect baseline—a bipartisan compromise unsupported by empirical evidence—was enough to sway the Supreme Court. Imagine what a better metric could achieve.

ELECTION ADMINISTRATION
A World without Data

The story of the photo ID looks a lot like the story of election reform generally. Reform battles take place in a world without data. We know more about the companies in which we invest, the performance of our local baseball team, even our dishwashers, than we do about how our election system is working. The institutions that administer our election system—the linchpin of any democracy—don't give us the information we need to evaluate how they are performing. The limited data that exist are often undependable, unverifiable, and too inconsistent to allow for comparisons across jurisdictions. It is remarkable that we spend so much time arguing about which direction election reform should take when we don't even have the data we need to map where we are now.

The Absence of Data

Consider a few remarkable facts. We do not know how many people *cast a ballot* during our last presidential election because 20 percent of the states do not report this information; they disclose only how many ballots were successfully counted.[16] We do not know how many voters stood in long lines. We do not know how many poll workers showed up to work. We do not know what percentage of voting machines broke down on Election Day.

Our data problems are so basic that in October 2004, the Caltech/MIT Voting Technology Project, composed of some of the most highly respected political scientists in the country, issued a plea for all states and localities to collect data on such rudimentary questions as the number of registered voters, the number of ballots cast, and the types of ballots included in the official count.[17] Four years later, we still don't have that information.

The data are so sparse that it is hard even to evaluate how much things have improved since the 2000 election. As Charles Stewart of MIT has observed, "For all the attention focused on the problem [of election administration] since November 2000 and all the money thrown at improving voting in the United States, it is impossible to demonstrate anything but the most basic improvements in voting, nationwide, using systematic data."[18]

The jurisdictions that do keep data often define basic terms differently. As the University of Utah's Thad Hall and Ohio State's Dan Tokaji have explained, states do not have "a common definition regarding what constitutes an early or absentee ballot."[19] Even the states that report residual vote rates—that elegant metric political scientists invented to assess balloting problems—record that number inconsistently. In category after category, cross-jurisdiction comparisons cannot be trusted because election administrators do not adhere to the same protocols for gathering information.

Even states that keep rudimentary data on election performance fail to record the information we need to identify problems and figure out solutions. For instance, most of the jurisdictions that keep information on how many ballots were cast but not counted cannot tell us *why* these ballot weren't counted. The same holds true for the registration process. As the Carter-Baker Commission found, "We still do not know how many people are unable to vote because their name is missing from the registration list or their identification was rejected at the polls. We also have no idea about the level of fraud or the accuracy and completeness of voter registration lists."[20]

If you need further evidence of the woeful state of the data, look no farther than the latest survey of state practices conducted by the Election Assistance Commission,[21] the federal agency charged with helping states improve how they administer federal elections.[22] In submitting three reports to Congress in 2007,[23] the EAC asked states for information on such important topics as voter registration, turnout, balloting, voting machines, and poll workers. A striking number of states simply did not report that information.

To get a sense of just how poor a job the states did in reporting, take a look at the following ranking.[24] It evaluates the states based on whether they disclosed information in 13 categories used by the EAC.[25] States were graded solely on the basis of reporting, with no judgment made as to the validity of the underlying data.[26] The ranking was derived by toting up the state's scores in each category and then averaging them. The percentage listed next to each state indicates what percentage of the EAC's requests were met by the state on a category-by-category basis.

Rank	*State*	*Score*
1	North Dakota	99.20%
2	Delaware	98.25%
3	Montana	97.37%
4	Georgia	96.41%
5	Florida	96.11%
6	Ohio	95.47%
7	Texas	91.80%
8	Michigan	90.23%
9	Arizona	85.46%
10	Alaska	84.21%
11	Wyoming	81.34%
12	Washington	81.24%
13	Maryland	75.13%
14	Missouri	74.19%
15	New Jersey	73.04%
16	Arkansas	71.04%

Rank	*State*	*Score*
17	Idaho	70.42%
18	Iowa	70.21%
19	Utah	69.77%
20	North Carolina	69.54%
21	Kentucky	69.22%
22	Colorado	67.70%
23	Nevada	66.83%
24	Louisiana	65.07%
25	Oregon	64.45%
26	South Dakota	62.58%
27	Mississippi	54.54%
28	New York	53.28%
29	Hawaii	52.93%
30	Kansas	52.62%
31	Oklahoma	51.87%
32	California	50.74%
33	Maine	49.63%
34	New Mexico	49.33%
35	Nebraska	47.64%
36	Rhode Island	46.77%
37	West Virginia	43.65%
38	Indiana	43.31%
39	Pennsylvania	42.00%
40	Minnesota	41.65%
41	Virginia	40.43%
42	Illinois	39.67%
43	Tennessee	38.16%

Rank	*State*	*Score*
44	South Carolina	33.02%
45	Connecticut	28.01%
46	Vermont	27.12%
47	Massachusetts	24.81%
48	Wisconsin	23.13%
49	New Hampshire	21.68%
50	Alabama	21.34%

Note: Hawaii contains five legally defined counties. One of them, Kalawao, contains approximately 147 people and is a designated leper colony in a state of quarantine. Most of the instances in which one of Hawaii's five counties failed to report requested data involved Kalawao. If that county is dropped from the calculations, Hawaii's score increases to 67.4 percent, which moves it from twenty-ninth on the ranking up to twenty-third. North Dakota is exempt from the National Voter Registration Act because it does not register voters. The ranking thus excludes NVRA survey items when scoring that state. If the NVRA survey items were included, North Dakota would fall to thirteen on the ranking.

The ranking is certainly not perfect.* As with all rankings, it involves discretionary judgments,[27] some of which I effectively "contracted out" by relying on the EAC's views about what mattered. Moreover, while there are good justifications for requesting each piece of information, some parts of the survey are more important than others for evaluating how well a system is performing. The ranking, however, weights disclosures based on the categories designated by the EAC (giving equal weight to each category), not on the basis of their relative importance. Needless to say, a differently weighted system would result in a different ranking.[28]

Despite these limitations (which I discuss in greater detail in chapters 4 and 5), the ranking at least gives us a rough sense of how poorly the states are doing in collecting data that the Election Assistance Commission thought it needed to fulfill its congressional mandate. For example, the ranking reveals that only thirteen states were able to report more than three-quarters of the information requested of them, and over half the state reported less than 60 percent of the survey items. If you dig down into the survey, you will see that the average response rate for each survey item ranged from 54 percent to 65 percent, and only fifteen of the ninety-two items contain complete or nearly complete data from the states.[29]

The ranking also reveals a remarkable level of variation in state reporting practices. Delaware and North Dakota had a nearly perfect reporting rate, but the lowest-ranked states—Massachusetts, Wisconsin, New Hampshire, and Alabama—disclosed less than one-quarter of the information the EAC requested of them. It is also hard to identify any obvious explanations for the states' disparate reporting practices. Wealthy states like Connecticut, Massachusetts, and New Hampshire ranked very low. Several states that tout themselves as "good governance" states (Vermont, Wisconsin) score poorly, whereas a few states that have recently experienced election fiascos (Ohio, Florida) rank quite high. With the exception of the exceptionally poor performance by New England, there also does not seem to be any clear regional pattern to the disclosure rate. Southern states, for instance, can be found at the top (Georgia) and bottom (Alabama) of the ranking. States with lots of jurisdictions (the New England states) tended to have low reporting rates, but other places did pretty while despite a fair number of reporting jurisdictions.

If you dig deeper into the data, the problems multiply.[30] For instance, Massachusetts reported that only 7.1 percent of its population participated in the 2006 election, well below any realistic turnout assessment. Fourteen states indicated that they received zero ballots from overseas military voters, a claim that is extremely hard to believe. States reported that they required between zero and 18,627 poll workers to show up for work on Election Day. Five claimed that they need fewer than five poll workers to staff the entire state! One state mysteriously claimed that only 300 poll workers are required, that 17,532 served, and yet that thirty-two polling places were nonetheless understaffed. Finally, despite estimates that we were missing one-quarter of the poll workers needed to staff our election system in 2004[31] and legions of reports about how difficult it is to recruit poll workers, only one state—Ohio—reported that the number of poll workers who showed up was less than the number of poll workers it required. Perhaps the other forty-nine states managed to eliminate recruitment challenges in just two years, but I suspect it is actually Ohio that should be commended here.

Worse still, what we see in the EAC report is actually a good deal better than what the states initially reported. Sometimes states did not even bother to fill in information. Others reported answers that were obviously wrong on their face. EAC staffers and consultants spent countless hours tracking down officials about their disclosures and pounding the data into shape. Even after all that effort, many states still failed to report all the data requested, and it is hard to draw state-by-state comparisons in many categories because of inconsistencies in reporting practices.

A COMPARATIVE VIEW

The Private Sector

To place these data-collection problems in perspective, it is worth considering how many public and private organizations have come to rely on data-driven policymaking. My colleague Ian Ayres has written about "supercrunchers" who use data-driven analysis to build sports teams, diagnose disease, evaluate loan risk, assess the quality of a new wine, predict the future price of plane tickets, calculate the likelihood that a parolee will commit another crime, choose which passenger will be bumped off an airline flight, and inform car dealers how far they can push a customer on price.[32]

Take Wal-Mart, for instance. Wal-Mart's database is gigantic; only the federal government keeps more data.[33] The company mines that data relentlessly to increase sales. For example, Wal-Mart's data revealed that bananas are the grocery item that its customers purchase most often. The company therefore made sure that bananas were available not just in the produce aisle, but near the cereal. Wal-Mart's data are so precise that it knows that strawberry Pop-Tarts sell at seven times their usual rate just before a hurricane. It now stocks not just extra flashlights, but boxes of Pop-Tarts, in advance of a storm.[34] Wal-Mart has similarly used data on customer satisfaction to identify where it could most easily improve, leading it to create faster checkout processes and cleaner stores.[35] Wal-Mart may represent an extreme example, but data-crunching and benchmarking are routine practices in Fortune 500 companies.

It's easy to see why. Would you invest in a company that kept as little performance data as election administrators collect? Imagine a corporation that didn't know how many people it employed, how many customers it had, or what percentage of its business came from Internet sales. (Many states and localities cannot tell you how many poll workers showed up on election day, how many people were registered to vote or cast a ballot during the last election, or what share of the ballots came from absentee or early voters.) Imagine a company that didn't know its customers' preferences or why they went elsewhere to make their purchases. (Election administrators generally don't survey voters about their voting experiences or keep track of how many voters tried to register and cast a ballot but failed.) Imagine a company that never sent testers to evaluate whether it was easy to navigate its stores or purchase its products, or one that failed to conduct regular audits of its accounting books. (Election administrators don't deploy testers to evaluate, and many fail to conduct adequate postelection audits.) Imagine that the corporation never engaged in the routine business practice of benchmarking—comparing its performance against other companies to identify where it could do better. (Benchmarking rarely occurs in the elections context.) Imagine a company that didn't know its own market share. (Election administrators often don't know what percentage of their jurisdiction's eligible citizens they serve.)

My guess is that you wouldn't invest a dime in the company I just described. So why are you willing to entrust the nation's most precious noncommodity—the vote—to an election system like ours?

You don't have to be a supercruncher to care about performance data. Think of something much simpler: buying a dishwasher. If you want to choose a dishwasher, *Consumer Reports* offers extensive comparative information about performance, price, and repair histories. Election officials, however, cannot give you comparable information about how well the state's registration system or ballot-counting process is working. Voting machines, of course, have received the greatest scrutiny. Researchers have generated some information about their reliability and performance,[36] though even here the data fall short.[37] In other areas, though, we have almost nothing to go on.

The Public Sector

Lest you think that data matter only to the private sector, government agencies at the state[38] and federal levels[39] routinely rely on data-driven analysis to improve their performance.[40] One of the best-known programs is called CitiStat, which was modeled on the Comstat program that brought the New York Police Department so much success.[41] CitiStat was first used in Baltimore with impressive results.[42] The city's mayor met regularly with department heads to create performance targets and assess progress toward them using data generated and collected by the city. For instance, the mayor decided that every pothole should be fixed within forty-eight hours of someone reporting it. The city then used performance data to evaluate its progress in reaching that goal.[43] Data-driven analysis has been used in a variety of public institutions, ranging from police departments[44] to housing agencies,[45] from transportation agencies[46] to education departments.[47]

Data-driven analysis has a long and distinguished historical pedigree as well. Just think about the vast amount of economic data that the government collects. We're all familiar with the GDP, which aggregates the value of goods and services over a set time period. The GDP has become a key metric for evaluating economic performance, providing a universal quantitative reference point for evaluating economic conditions.

The GDP gives us the snapshot that Gary Smith, the businessman turned election official, insists on having whenever he starts a new job. It maps where we are and helps us chart our future path. For instance, when the GDP shows a particular level of decline, we know we are in a recession, a diagnosis that prompts policy responses to jumpstart the economy. In the nineteenth century, in sharp contrast, economic downturns often prompted panics. As the name suggests, the term refers to "'a sudden fright without cause,'"[48] an apt description for a financial crisis that occurs in a world without aggregate economic data. In a world without data, it's hard to tell the difference between a genuine problem and a statistical glitch, between a recession and a random economic dip.

The economy isn't the only area where our government constantly measures. We conduct a full-blown census every ten years. Almost one hundred federal agencies boast data-collection programs.[49] We collect statistics on the environment, transportation, crime, prisons, farming, disease, housing, childcare, immigration, aging, patents, the labor market, international development, medical services, imports and exports, and gas prices. We even try to measure things that many people believe can't be measured, like the quality of a public education.

Election Administration: The Mysterious Outlier

Given how pervasive data-driven policymaking is, the mystery is why something that so naturally lends itself to measurement—election performance—is barely measured at all. Most of the arguments against data-driven analysis—debates over the widespread use of CitiStat by government agencies, the *U.S. News and World Report* rankings, No Child Left Behind—boil down to a worry that institutional performance can't be measured. People argue, with some justification, that quantitative measures can't possibly capture how well a school educates its students or whether the government is providing the right social services.

The main thrust of these arguments is that gauging institutional performance requires us to make value judgments, and data can't make those judgments for us. Data-driven analysis may be a natural tool in the business arena, some argue, because the goal is clear: businesses are supposed to make money. Government agencies and educational institutions, in contrast, are supposed to carry out a variety of tasks that necessarily require more complex normative assessments.

While it is plainly true that judging election performance requires us to make value-laden decisions about what matters and why, as I explain in chapters 4 and 5, some government activities lend themselves more easily to measurement than others. Election data fall on the comfortable end of this sliding scale. People call election administration practices the "nuts and bolts" with good reason. These aren't the issues that have riven those who want to improve elections, like campaign finance or felon disenfranchisement. Even if the parties have a tendency to play politics on some issues, there's actually a good deal of agreement on how an election system should work. Moreover, much of what we value in election administration can be captured in a statistic: how long were the lines? how many ballots got discarded? how often did the machines break down? how many people complained about their poll workers?

We haven't yet had the debate about numbers that has already occurred in the many areas of governance where policymakers have turned to quantitative evidence to inform their decisions, and it would take an entire book to rehash those arguments here. Nonetheless, based on the results of those debates thus far, it is hard to imagine that election administration won't end up moving toward a greater reliance on quantitative data. After all, it is hard to make the case that election administration involves more complex normative judgments than are made in the vast swaths of our lives—employment, health, education—where policymakers have decided that numbers are necessary. It is harder still to argue that the normative judgments we are already making in election administration should not be informed by good data.

THE NEW FACE OF ENVIRONMENTAL REFORM

I began this chapter with Spencer Overton's story, a tale about new-style reformer struggling with an old problem. Now let me tell you about Dan Esty. Think of the word *environmentalist* and the first image that springs to mind may be your college roommate who recycled everything or Tiva-shod baby boomers trying save the polar bear. Dan Esty, a professor of environmental law and policy at Yale, is nothing like the stereotype. Clad in a well-tailored suit, porting the latest in cell phone technology, he speaks in the clipped sentences of a corporate executive. It is easy to imagine him in his first job as a trade lawyer at a top-flight Washington law firm. Though Esty is more than capable of talking idealistically about why environmental reform matters, he usually sounds more like a McKinsey consultant than a Sierra Club member. His arguments are punctuated by phrases you won't hear at an Earth Day celebration: performance goals, data-driven analysis, action items, benchmarking, leveraging, and competition. In an area dominated by starry-eyed idealists, Esty's style is that of a hardheaded corporative executive.[50]

Esty's style is also what makes him so effective. He's the rare environmentalist who has the ear of big business. That's because Esty has always had one foot in the world of reform and the other in the world of business. When Esty was a young lawyer, he divided his time between pro bono environmental clients and paying trade clients. He quickly noticed that the two groups were always talking past one another. Like Overton, Esty serves the role of translator between two worlds. His first book was devoted to casting environmental claims in terms that trade policymakers could understand.[51]

In working on that project, Esty realized that environmentalists have a problem. If you want to improve the environment, business matters. But businesspeople are exceedingly skeptical of reformers. It isn't just a question of language. Businesspeople often worry that environmentalists haven't come to grips with the costly trade-offs associated with reform, and they get irritated with what Esty calls reformers' "holier-than-thou-ness." Esty also believes that environmentalists have as much to learn from businesspeople as businesspeople do from environmentalists. However, routine business practices like data-driven analysis and benchmarking were simply "not the ethos of the environmental culture."[52]

Esty's vision of data-driven reform crystallized when he attended the 1998 meeting of the World Economic Forum in Davos. There he was struck by the success of the Forum's Global Competitiveness Index, which ranks countries based on their potential for economic growth.[53] It was clear that the ranking mattered a great deal to the business and governmental leaders gathered there. Esty could also trace its effects on economic policies throughout the world.

Esty worried that the Global Competitiveness Index captured only part of the story. It did not provide similar comparative data on countries' environmental performance. That meant that nation-states were competing fiercely to move up the rankings on the financial side but feeling no pressure to do so on the environmental side. Esty's mantra is that "what matters gets measured,"[54] and environmental performance wasn't being measured.

Esty and a group of environmentalists at the conference came up with a plan to rank countries based on their environmental performance. With the support of a philanthropist and academic centers at Columbia and Yale, they pulled together publicly available environmental data to create what has become the Environmental Performance Index.[55] The EPI ranks 149 countries along twenty-five performance indicators. It allows us to make detailed comparisons of the progress nation-states have made in promoting human health and protecting the ecosystem.

Remember when I asked you at the end of Spencer Overton's story to imagine what a reliable yardstick for judging election reform debates could achieve? Dan Esty can tell you exactly what such a metric can achieve. The EPI has affected environmental debates across the globe. Consider what occurred in Belgium after the first version of the Environmental Performance Index was released. Belgian environmentalists had long tried to persuade legislators that the country's environmental practices were subpar. But without any concrete, comparative information on performance, all environmentalists in Belgium could do was exhort the government to do more or engage policymakers in complex discussions well beyond the grasp of most citizens. These debates about inputs (funding levels, regulatory choices) had gotten nowhere.

When the EPI showed that Belgium fell well below its European counterparts on the ranking system—roughly in the same range as Cameroon, Mozambique, and Albania[56]—the conversation changed. The story made headlines in the country's major newspapers, and reformers suddenly had a rather large stick to beat legislators into doing something. Government officials could go on and on about the merits of Belgian policies. But they could not dispute the bottom line: Belgium was not keeping up with its peers along a wide range of performance measures. The EPI precipitated a sizable political crisis in Belgium, and the result was genuine reform.

Or take the example of South Korea. It ranks forty-second on the 2006 EPI.[57] Eager to improve its standing, South Korea has assembled a team of thirty people—at a cost of roughly $5 million a year—to figure out how to do better. By way of comparison, Esty's team is composed of ten people and spends about $1 million each year to put the ranking together.[58]

The aggregate numbers measuring the EPI's influence are equally impressive. There have been one million hits on the EPI website. More than sixty governments have consulted with the EPI team about improving their environmental policies. And the push toward quantification appears to be taking root among environmentalists, as others have tried to find sensible, easily communicated measures of environmental performance. Some environmentalists, for instance, now challenge individuals and businesses to improve their carbon footprint, which measures energy consumption in units of carbon dioxide.[59]

The EPI is clearly a here-to-there strategy. It does not mandate a particular policy or set any regulatory baselines. Instead, it helps change the conversation about environmental reform, creating incentives for policymakers to do the right thing. The result is that, at least in some places, environmental reform has taken root.

Esty is quite clear about why the EPI has worked. It packages environmental concerns in the language of business, providing policymakers and voters hard data and comparative benchmarks to assess their nation's performance. Esty notes that when the EPI was first created, people were "shocked that you could put hard numbers to environmental performance."[60]

According to Esty, the numbers matter. A ranking enables reformers to distill a wide-ranging set of concerns into something accessible to—and noticed by—the press and top-level governing officials. Reports by environmental reform groups tend to get relatively little press. The EPI regularly makes headlines. Most environmental reformers spend their time lobbying legislators or cajoling bureaucrats. Esty's group meets regularly with prime ministers and presidents.

A performance ranking also helps reformers and policymakers pinpoint problems and identify where they can do better. As Esty notes, it is a commonplace among corporate executives that "accounting gives context for choice."[61] Environmental accounting serves a similar purpose. The conventional model for environmental reform, Esty says, is "guru-based decisionmaking,"[62] which relies on movement heroes to articulate a platform. That approach succeeded in the early days of the environmental movement, says Esty, because there was a lot of "low-hanging fruit"—virtually any proposal represented an improvement on the status quo. But Esty thinks that regulatory choices are harder today than they were twenty-five years ago, and the demand that governments "do better, do more" is no longer enough to convince policymakers.[63]

Hard, comparative data have also given environmentalists a better sense of the drivers of performance. There has been a long debate among environmentalists as to what matters most for environmental performance: money? strong regulations? enforcement? capacity building? Everyone had an intuition, but it was hard to figure out whose intuitions were correct. The EPI has moved us one step closer to an answer by providing data that can be used to figure out what correlates with strong environmental performance. The conventional wisdom was that money matters, that rich countries always do a better job of protecting the environment than poor ones. Because the EPI keeps track not just of performance outputs (ozone measures, child mortality rates, air quality assessments) but policy inputs (economic wealth, good governance), Esty and his team can test the conventional wisdom. Regression analysis suggests that the conventional wisdom is only partially right. Rich countries generally do better than poor countries on the EPI. But there is a good deal of variation within both groups, and that variation seems to be driven largely by good-governance factors, like strong environmental regulations, protections against corruption, and public debate over environmental issues. To be sure, we are far from having a definitive answer about what drives environmental reform (and the question itself is too complex to measure with absolute confidence). Nonetheless, the Environmental Performance Index has at least helped reformers get a preliminary read on these issues.

THE IMPORTANCE OF DATA-DRIVEN POLICYMAKING

In the next chapter, I'll argue that the world would look quite different if election reformers like Spencer Overton possessed the same tool that Dan Esty wields. Before turning to that discussion, however, I want to move beyond Overton's story and talk more generally about what election reform debates look like in today's environment.

The problem with reform battles in a world without data is that we all end up acting too much like Lev Tolstoy's coachmen. When there's no evidence to analyze, there's not much left to do but shout. For too many election issues, we are in exactly the same position as Spencer Overton or the Carter-Baker Commission or Justice Stevens. We lack the information we need to be confident that we've correctly identified the problem and chosen the right solution. We argue incessantly about which path election reform should take even though no one can even map where we are right now.

Photo ID is a question to which most election reformers think that the Carter-Baker Commission and the Supreme Court got the wrong answer. But reformers make plenty of claims that aren't supported by empirical evidence. They don't have much of a choice. Without good data, there is not much but intuition and anecdote to go on. Commonsense intuitions can get you reasonably far, but at some point the absence of data calls into question the basic facts on which those intuitions are based. As Ohio State's Dan Tokaji argued in a rather pointed rebuke the reform community, "Efforts at election reform have been based on an intuition-based approach . . . [that] places too much weight on seat-of-the-pants assessments of what makes for good elections."[64]

It is not surprising that Tokaji is acutely aware of the shortcomings of the current debate. He's a baseball nut. When Tokaji isn't teaching election law, he's traveling around the country in his quest to see a baseball game in every stadium in the country. Don't even try to talk to him about the Red Sox. Legend has it that he threatened to toss his roommate, a Mets fan, out the window during the heartbreaking 1986 World Series. And Dan's been a lot happier since the Red Sox hired Bill James, the number guru whom many credit with the Sox's recent success.

Baseball, of course, is an American institution where statistics have always mattered. As sportswriter Roger Angell notes, "Every player in every game is subjected to a cold and ceaseless accounting; no ball is thrown and no base is gained without an instant responding judgment—ball or strike, hit or error, yea or nay—and an ensuing statistic."[65] Supercrunchers like Bill James have played an increasingly important role in the sport, as Michael Lewis documents in *Moneyball: The Art of Winning an Unfair Game.*[66] There Lewis describes the success of the Oakland A's, whose management drastically improved the team's performance by hiring based on hard, comparative data instead of the gut-level judgments of baseball scouts.

Drawing on Lewis's book, Tokaji argues that we need to take a "moneyball" approach to election reform.[67] He writes that arguments for election reform have too often been based on the same approach as "the old-time scouts in Lewis's book, ... neglecting serious empirical research into what works and doesn't work in the real world."[68] Tokaji says we need "hard data and rigorous analysis" in place of "the anecdotal approach that has too often dominated election reform conversations."[69]

A Democracy Index fits neatly with Tokaji's moneyball approach. Rather than focusing on necessarily atmospheric judgments about what problems exist, the Index would provide concrete, comparative data on bottom-line results. It would allow us to figure out not just what is happening in a given state or locality, but how its performance compares to similarly situated jurisdictions'. It would help us spot, surface, and solve the problems that afflict our system. The Democracy Index would, in short, give us the same diagnostic tool used routinely by corporations and government agencies to figure out what's working and what's not.

Identifying Problems and Solutions

The absence of good data poses the most basic of dilemmas for those who care about reform: it is hard to figure out whether and where problems exist in a world without information. Election experts can name the symptoms they see routinely; even the haphazard information available now reveals this much. But if you were to identify a specific election system and ask whether the problem existed there, experts might not be able to answer your question. Problems are hard to pinpoint in a world without data.

For example, we would presumably be worried if a large number of people tried to cast a ballot in the last presidential but failed to do so. It might be a sign that registration systems weren't functioning properly, that poll workers were doing a bad job, that ballots were designed poorly, or that machines were not working well. Yet 20 percent of states cannot even tell you how many people cast a ballot that wasn't counted, let alone how many were turned away before they filled out a ballot.

Remember Conny McCormack, who just retired as the county clerk/recorder-registrar of Los Angeles County? She has been better situated than most election officials to identify cost-effective strategies for reducing the number of lost ballots. The reason is simple: L.A. County keeps better data than most states and localities. Her staff routinely tracked not just how many ballots were cast but not counted, but *why* ballots weren't counted. For instance, McCormack could tell you how many absentee ballots weren't counted because they arrived after the deadline, lacked a necessary signature, or were returned as undeliverable.

Because L.A. County tracks these numbers, McCormack was able to identify when she had a problem. For instance, early on in her tenure, McCormack and her staff realized that a large number of absentee ballots weren't counted because they arrived after the deadline. Taking a look at the packets sent to voters, McCormack realized that the deadline was announced only inside the packet. She and her staff then redesigned the envelope so that it informed voters in red letters when the ballot had to be received. By placing this information in a more prominent place for voters, L.A. County was able to reduce the number of absentee ballots that were disqualified on timing grounds. It was a simple, virtually cost-free solution.

There are many examples where data have helped election administrators do a better job. Take Bob Murphy, who is Maryland's Electronic Poll Book Project monitor.[70] A poll book is what election staff use to check you in when you vote. Murphy, a computer junkie, realized that Maryland's new electronic poll books contained extremely helpful information on turnout patterns. "We always knew who voted before," says Murphy, "but now we know *when* they voted." When Murphy started playing around with the data, he realized that people's voting patterns depended on things like where they lived and how old they were. The elderly, for instance, tend to vote midmorning, which means you'll want to staff up polling places in areas with large elderly populations during those periods. Murphy even discovered that the "conventional wisdom" that there's a noontime rush in polling places is true only for a small percentage of Maryland's polling sites. Armed with four elections' worth of data, Murphy can figure out exactly how much equipment and staff he needs in a given precinct to prevent lines from developing.

Gary Smith, the businessman turned election administrator, has also put data on turnout patterns to good use. Like many election administrators, Smith has to figure out "how to disperse my assets in a more efficient way."

He's not only used data on turnout patterns to distribute his voting machines efficiently, but to ensure that every community in his jurisdiction receives equal service, not just an equal number of machines.[71] For instance, Smith has mapped the residence of all the people who vote early in one of Forsyth County's early voting sites.[72] He's thus able to make sure that the early voting sites are serving every community equally. Moreover, Smith can tell when an early voting site is being underused and fix the problem (perhaps by providing better signage or switching locations). Those adjustments don't just make it easier for Atlanta residents to vote. They reduce the number of people who vote absentee. Because absentee ballots are more expensive to process than early votes, Smith's adjustments have a direct effect on his office's bottom line.

Joe Mansky, the scientist turned election administrator, has used data to improve the design of Minnesota ballots. Badly designed ballots lead voters to make mistakes when they vote; they can vote for the wrong candidate (remember Palm Beach County's infamous butterfly ballot?) or cast an invalid ballot. Mansky oversaw one of the earliest rollouts of optical scan machines, and there were a lot of questions about how best to design an optical scan ballot at the time. By gathering data during the early stages of the process, his staff learned how to fashion the ballots so that voters made fewer mistakes in marking them.[73]

Distinguishing between a Glitch and a Trend

Even when we can identify a potential problem with good data, it's hard to figure out where that problem looms largest or to distinguish between a statistical blip and a genuine pattern. Tammy Patrick, an election administrator for Maricopa County in Arizona, can tell you a lot about distinguishing between glitches and trends. Like most people in election administration, Patrick fell into the job through some combination of happenstance and interest. Most of her career was spent working in sales in the private sector. Patrick was eventually tapped to be Maricopa's federal compliance officer at a time when the county was tussling with the Department of Justice over federal language assistance requirements. The county eventually agreed to create a program to track compliance with those provisions. But Patrick thought that it could do much more. Why not create a system that could track election problems of *all* types?

When Patrick came up with the idea, voter complaints were all tracked on slips of paper. Patrick and her coworkers created an online database for tracking complaints in real time. Patrick's sales experience paid off here. She made sure that the software "prepopulated" data and minimized the number of keystrokes needed to enter a complaint. The resulting program has been a great success, earning the county national recognition. It not only allows the staff to dispatch troubleshooters to deal with discrete problems, but provides for systemwide solutions when the data reveal a troubling trend. Maricopa's reporting system doesn't just allow for midcourse corrections. It also serves as a long-term diagnostics tool so that county officials who evaluate employee performance can do a better job of training going forward.

I asked Patrick to give me an example of how her system worked. She told me to imagine that I'd gotten a report from Precinct X—the ink had run dry in the pens voters need to fill in their ballots (a reasonably common problem in a desert community). Maybe it's a glitch (perhaps that's the precinct where the pens sat in the hot delivery truck the longest, so I can fix the problem just by sending a new box of pens there). Maybe it's a trend (the manufacturer sent bad pens, and the problem is going to shut down the voting process). Needless to say, I'd want to find out quickly whether it's a glitch or a trend. "We can do that in real time," she noted proudly.

Benchmarking

The secret to Tammy Patrick's idea is that it provides the right information in the right form. As Patrick recognized, a reporting system is a good start, but those bits of data are most useful if they are pulled together into a usable form.

The Democracy Index is Tammy Patrick's idea writ large. Good policy requires something more than a bunch of individual jurisdictions collecting data on their own performance. It requires us to benchmark. Benchmarking is a routine practice in the business world, as corporations constantly compare their performance with that of their competitors to identify best practices and figure out where they can improve.

Most of the benchmarking studies we have were done by social scientists, who wangled enough funding to gather the necessary data. But those studies are inherently limited. They tend to be small-scale and focus on narrow questions. More importantly, they cannot provide grounds for drawing conclusions across widely varying jurisdictions. Election administration is too complex and too varied to be captured by studying a small sample. As several scholars have explained, an election system is like an "ecosystem": "Changes in any one part of the system are likely to affect other areas, sometimes profoundly."[74] When ecosystems vary as much as they do in the elections context, large-scale, cross-jurisdictional studies are essential.

Put differently, election reformers and policymakers today function a lot like doctors did in the old days. Based on limited information they have about the symptoms of the problem (lots of ballots are discarded, the lines seem long), they try to identify the underlying disease (is the problem badly trained poll workers? malfunctioning machinery?). Like the doctors of yore, election reformers and administrators may even try one fix, followed by another, hoping that their educated guesses turn out to be correct. The problem is that their educated guesses are still just that—guesses.

Even when someone comes up with a good guess as to a solution, we can't tell how much improvement it will bring or how its effects would compare to other, less costly solutions. In today's environment of tight budgets and limited resources, this lack of precision undermines the case for change.

What we need is what modern medicine provides: large-scale, comparative studies that tell us what works and what doesn't. The Democracy Index is a first step in that direction. It would provide comparative data regarding both policy inputs (registration practices, balloting rules, training programs) and performance outputs (data on discarded ballots, the length of lines, the number of voter complaints). Those numbers would allow us to run the large, cross-jurisdictional studies that we need to identify best practices.

Figuring Out What Drives Performance

The dearth of data doesn't just make it hard to cure specific ailments in our election system. It also prevents us from inoculating the system against future disease. Put yourselves in the shoes of a reformer or an election administrator and you can see why comparative data are crucial. While you are certainly interested in specific fixes for discrete problems, you really want a robust system capable of self-correction so that problems can be avoided rather than corrected. You want to identify not just best practices, but the basic drivers of performance.

If you are interested in the drivers of performance, absolute numbers matter to you, but comparative numbers are far more useful. After all, if you can't even identify who's doing well, it is hard to figure out precisely what drives good performance. Without comparative data on performance, we cannot know whether, for instance, well-funded systems tend to succeed, or whether the key is centralization, better training, or nonpartisan administration.[75] Because the Democracy Index ranks states and localities based on overall performance, it provides precisely the comparative information we need.

CONCLUSION

Whether we are arguing about discrete policy solutions or the drivers of performance, too much of the debate takes place in a world without data. The Democracy Index would help address this problem by giving us the same tool that doctors, businessmen, and now environmentalists possess: comparative information on bottom-line results. By providing the right information in the right form, the Index would enable reformers and election administrators to figure out which jurisdictions do well in individual categories and which ones run the best systems overall.

The Democracy Index is especially intriguing because it would help turn one of the biggest obstacles to reform—decentralization—into an advantage. Academics like to tell you that one of the benefits of decentralization is that it allows states and localities to function as "laboratories of democracy,"[76] with different jurisdictions coming up with different solutions for the same problem. But there is little point to having laboratories of democracy if no one reports the results of the experiments.

If the Democracy Index did nothing more than give us a map—helping us identify where we are and figure out where we want to go—it would represent a significant improvement on the status quo. At the very least, we'd have some confidence in our assessment of the problems we face (the "here") and the solutions we should pursue (the "there"). But the Index has the potential to do a good deal more than that. It has the potential to help us get from there to there, a subject to which I turn in the next chapter.

3 The Politics of Reform and the Promise of Ranking

In the last chapter, I offered a tale of two reformers. Spencer Overton fights for election reform in a world without data. Dan Esty battles for environmental change with an important weapon: an index that ranks countries based on performance. In this chapter, I'll explain why the Democracy Index could provide a similarly powerful tool for election reformers. Indeed, if we focus on the key leverage points in the reform process—voters, policymakers, and election administrators—it is clear that a Democracy Index could do a great deal to smooth the path for change.

VOTERS AS LEVERAGE POINTS

Realigning Partisan and Local Incentives

Voters are a key leverage point in the reform process. We wouldn't worry about partisanship or local competition if voters pressured elected officials to do the right thing. Unfortunately, it is often tough for reform proposals to get traction with voters. That might seem strange given that the word *democracy* is invoked with reverence by schoolchildren and politicians alike. Everyone is affected by a badly run system. So why aren't voters energized about these issues?[1]

Framing the Issue

While voters care about how elections are run, discussions about reform are largely inaccessible to them. In most policy debates, voters need a "frame"[2] to help them understand the problem and get behind a solution. Just think about how the 2008 presidential candidates framed difficult policy issues like health care coverage or the U.S. policy in Iraq. Reformers, of course, are engaged in precisely the same endeavor. By providing stories, slogans, and analogies, reformers tee up issues for voters and develop constituencies for change.

Most election issues are hard to frame for voters. The discussion either takes place at such a high level of generality that people have no sense of what ought to be done, or it descends into a sea of incomprehensible detail that would try the patience of even the wonkiest voter.

When reformers make their pitch, they often speak in stirring terms, invoking democracy, the dignity of the ballot, the right to vote. You can practically hear the National Anthem playing in the background. This is all well and good, but the National Anthem doesn't give a citizen much to go on. Moreover, everyone can play the patriotism game; you can expect election officials will also claim the moral high ground and accuse the other side of neglecting fundamental principles. As any parent knows, it is hard to resolve an argument whose basic rhetorical structure is some variant of "am not, are too."

Things are little better when reformers and election officials swoop from these lofty heights to what election scholars call "the weeds." Reformers "have to talk mostly in generalities," observes Jonah Goldman of the National Campaign for Fair Elections, because the underlying policy debates seem so "dull."[3] The subject matter is arcane. Fights often involve intricate debates about counting ballots, jargon-filled discussions of election machinery, and disputes about nitty-gritty registration requirements. Even election junkies rarely have the stomach for it.

More importantly, these are debates that voters have no yardstick for judging. Reformers point to a problem—an inadequate registration system, outdated machinery, a poor system for training poll workers—and argue that the state can do better. Election officials respond by talking about regulations issued, resources allocated, and staff trained. Reformers talk about discarded ballots or unregistered voters. Election officials assure us these numbers are normal.

For voters, these debates are reminiscent of that famous *Far Side* cartoon entitled "What Dogs Hear." The clueless owner prattles away to his pet, and all the dog hears is "——, ——, ——, Ginger. ——, ——, Ginger, ——." So what do voters hear when reformers and administrators go at it?

A stream of technical details, occasionally punctuated with grand terms like *the right to vote* or *democracy*.

Voters are not stupid.[4] But none of us is born into the world with a strongly held intuition about whether optical scan systems are a good idea, or whether provisional ballots should be counted only if they are cast in the correct precinct. Voters are in the same position as the Supreme Court justices were in the voter ID case. They need a yardstick to help them figure out who's right.

The atmospherics of election reform do little to help the cause. In the absence of a reliable yardstick, voters' only strategy for resolving these debates is to pick someone to trust. But neither side is likely to engender widespread confidence. On one side you have elected politicians and embattled bureaucrats, whose pleas that they are doing the best they can are as likely to elicit cynicism as sympathy from the electorate. On the other side of the debate are election-reform advocates, who are often branded with the same stereotypes attached to other reformers: idealistic, liberal, naive. In private, election reformers are about as cynical as anyone can get about politics. In public, their mantra—"Do better, do more"—is the same one environmentalists used before people like Dan Esty arrived on the scene. Even if reformers start to get any traction in these debates, there is a good chance that the political party in power, fiercely protective of its privileges, will label them as partisan zealots or sore losers.[5]

The Democracy Index could help change these dynamics by giving voters a yardstick to judge these fights. First, it gives voters the right information. Rather than bogging voters down in technical details about how the ideal system would be run or making vague assertions that we could do better, reformers could give voters information on something they can evaluate: bottom-line results.

Second, the Democracy Index presents the information in the right form by distilling the data into a highly intuitive, accessible format: a ranking. Moreover, because the Index grades election systems "on a curve"—measuring them against one another instead of some ideal standard—voters can feel confident that they are rewarding those who have succeeded while holding those on the bottom rung to a realistic standard of performance.

The Democracy Index ought to shift the rhetoric of reform debates, allowing starry-eyed idealists to speak in the pragmatic cadence of corporate executives. In place of anecdote and idealism, reformers could offer cold, hard statistics about a locality's performance. Rather than relying on abstract invocations of the right to vote or bogging down voters in the technical details, reformers could let the numbers speak for themselves. The Democracy Index would thus expand the reformers' vocabulary, enabling them to speak more concretely about trade-offs and second-best solutions and to appeal to business-minded ideas like accountability and competition.

Jumpstarting grassroots organizing. The most optimistic hope for the Index is that it will encourage voters to get more engaged with grassroots activities. It is not surprising that voters have been passive about election reform until now. Current debates put voters in a situation where they have nothing to contribute. Everyone can invoke the same vague generalities about the right to vote. But if voters are going to talk about policy, they'll have to spend their weekends reading the posts on electionline.org or the Caltech/MIT Voting Technology Project website instead of wiling away those hours watching Extreme Ironing,[6] the U.S. Rock/Paper/Scissors League,[7] or the Canadian Mixed Curling Championship.[8] To put this less facetiously, ask yourself this question: If the average voter had some impulse to write her representative or call a radio talk show or organize a petition drive, what exactly would she say?[9]

Ranking systems are useful because, as Dan Esty observes, they "democratize who can render an opinion."[10] (Whether you think the opinion is properly informed is a different question, explored in chapter 4.) Everyone can express a view on whether his state ought to be ranked higher than forty-fifth on the Democracy Index. By giving voters an issue they can wrap their hands around, it may be possible to get voters exercised about election reform. After all, the rare instances in which voters have gotten engaged with grassroots organizing—paper trails, voter ID—have all involved issues that appeal to people's intuitions.

The Democracy Index would also expand the grassroots organizer's time frame. In a world without data, the only time people are riled up about reform is when there's a crisis. Once a winner is picked, the media coverage that keeps voters engaged ends abruptly. Reformers thus have a very short time to organize a coalition for change. An Index, however, ensures that the reform remains salient long after a crisis (and even in its absence). A ranking creates a durable reminder that a problem exists. By expanding the organizer's time horizon, the Index may help build support for change over the long haul.

Giving Voters an Information Shortcut

Even if the Democracy Index does not spawn new grassroots organizing, we would at least expect it to help voters do something that they *already* do: cast a vote. The great advantage of ranking systems is that they offer voters an information shortcut for holding elected officials accountable for their missteps. Creating a new shorthand for voters ought to affect the political incentives that currently run against reform.

Against shorthand? Some might well bristle at the idea of voters' using shorthand to evaluate the way our elections are run. Shorthand, of course, is always an imperfect substitute for informed decision-making. Skeptics might worry that a ranking system is so simple as to be simplistic. Why not present voters with a full range of information rather than "spoon-feed" them a ranking?

Though the concern is well taken, it misstates the question. The choice is not between "spoon feeding" voters or providing them with a full buffet of information. Voters will inevitably use some sort of shorthand in casting a ballot. The choice is what kind of shorthand to supply.

Consider, for instance, how most voters cast their ballots. They usually know very little about the substantive positions of the candidates they elect.[11] Yet voters make surprisingly good decisions about how to cast a vote. Their decisions are by no means perfect and reveal predictable biases. But voters have figured out a pretty good strategy for choosing a candidate without sorting through the huge amount of information relevant to that decision.

How do voters do it? They use the party label as a shorthand—what political scientists would term a "heuristic"—in choosing a candidate.[12] The label *Democrat* or *Republican* functions like a Good Housekeeping Seal of Approval. It tells the voter that the candidate in question subscribes to values or policy preferences that are close enough to the voter's to choose him.[13] As several scholars have explained, if a voter "knows the big thing about the parties, he does not need to know all the little things."[14]

Political scientists have devoted a lot of energy to making party cues function more effectively for a simple reason: they are a good deal better than the other types of shorthand voters might use.[15] Without the party heuristic, voters would be more likely to base their votes on something unappetizing, such as a candidate's race or gender. Or they might cast ballots randomly so that voter preferences are disconnected from electoral outcomes. The basic defense of party labels is not that they are perfect—far from it—but that they are the best thing we've got. If you ask a political scientist whether it is a good idea for voters to rely on party cues, the likely response will be a sarcastic, "As opposed to what?"

If we think about that question here, a ranking system looks a good deal more appealing. Think about the proxies voters are likely to use today in casting their vote for election officials. The best bets seem to be (1) anecdotal evidence, (2) news about a widely reported crisis, or (3) partisan cues. For all its potential shortcomings, a ranking system is superior to each of these alternatives.

Anecdotal evidence is, of course, just that. While a bewildering number of academics think that what their taxi driver said on the drive to the conference constitutes reputable proof, a glitch here and there is not good evidence of a full-fledged problem. A ranking system, in contrast, focuses voters on the bigger picture, directing their attention to systemic concerns instead of the modest anomalies that can afflict even well-run systems. It also directs their attention to the good as well as the bad and the ugly, revealing which states and localities have done an especially impressive job of running elections.

Even evidence of a crisis may not be a useful guide for voters. While the worst-run systems are more vulnerable to a crisis, not all badly run systems will experience one. Indeed, given the dearth of the data, we cannot definitively rule out the possibility that recent brouhahas have happened in relatively well-run systems, places that just happened to be in the path of a turnout tsunami. Crisis-based voting also has the flavor of closing the barn door after the horse has been stolen. Voters need a tool that will help them prevent crises rather than merely react to them.

Finally, partisan cues don't provide a dependable heuristic for voters in this context. A party label can tell a voter whether a candidate is liberal or conservative, something that may map on to particular approaches to campaign finance or felon disenfranchisement. But in choosing an election administrator, voters need shorthand for evaluating professionalism and performance, and the party cue does not help. Democrats and Republicans are equally susceptible to running elections badly.

For all of these reasons, the Democracy Index has the potential to provide voters with a much-needed shorthand for casting a vote. By conveying information about the "big thing" in election administration—a rough sense of how well the system performs overall—it enables voters to make sensible decisions without knowing all of "the little things" buried in the data.

If the Democracy Index provides voters with a useable shorthand, it ought to generate a new political dynamic in the reform environment.[16] The current system offers politicians and local officials few reasons to pay attention to reform issues. You can bet that will change if votes start to turn on performance.

Realigning partisan incentives. Consider, for instance, the fate of Ohio's secretary of state, Kenneth Blackwell, whose travails were described in chapter 1. In 2006, Blackwell ran for governor. Imagine if Ted Strickland, the Democrat running against him, could have shown that Ohio was one of the worst-run election systems in the country. Surely Strickland would have trumpeted those results whenever he could. You can also be sure that secretaries of state across country would take notice of that campaign.

An Index would also be invoked by election officials whose systems rank high. Candidates are always on the hunt for something to distinguish them from their opponents, some theme to attract voters' attention. We see lots of examples of this type of self-promotion with other rankings. For instance, the latest release of the Government Performance Project, which grades state management practices, prompted immediate press releases by the governors of the top-ranked states.[17]

The Index won't only matter during the campaign season. It's also likely to be used in any recount battle. Parties wage recount wars on two fronts. In court, the parties' job is to get their ballots counted and their opponents' excluded. Any lawyer worth her salt will try to introduce the Index into evidence if it helps her case.

Parties also battle in the arena of public opinion, trying to enlist voters in their effort to win the legal battle and score political points. It's hard to imagine that neither party would invoke the Democracy Index in framing the recount debate for public consumption. After all, if the state ranked low, it would provide further evidence that the party in power failed to do its job properly. Conversely, if the state generally scored high on the Index, the party in power could use it as a shield against the accusations being levied by its opponents.

Should the Democracy Index be deployed in either context, it ought to help raise public awareness about the need for reform and create incentives for politicians to get behind it. If there's any lesson to be drawn from successful efforts at election reform in other countries, it is that the most effective proponent of reform is usually the opposing party. When the party out of power has a weapon—an advisory commission report, a judicial ruling, a ranking system—it will use it to beat on the other party at every opportunity. It's ugly, but effective.

Even setting aside political races and recount wars, one can imagine other ways in which the Index might be used as a sword or shield in partisan politics. For instance, election officials at the bottom of the list might be vulnerable to targeted fund-raising or get-out-the-vote organizing by political blogs (Daily Kos or RedState). Similarly, any politician dissatisfied with an election rule would surely invoke the Index. The Index, after all, makes an instance of special pleading look like a defense of the public interest.

For all of these reasons, the Democracy Index should hang like a sword of Damocles over politicians, a notoriously risk-averse group. While it will not be salient in every race, it should matter in some. That would mean that at least some of the time, the fate of elections officials would hinge in part on their professional performance, not just their party standing. Instead of asking an election official to stop thinking about her political interests in administering the election process, the Democracy Index links her political fate to her professional performance.

Would party heuristics trump? A skeptic might still insist that the party heuristic—whether someone has an *R* or *D* by her name—is all that really matters for low-salience campaigns like races for the secretary of state.[18] The worry is that party labels will drown out any competing information about candidates except during well-publicized campaigns for higher office, like Kenneth Blackwell's gubernatorial campaign. But even if partisan heuristics generally trump all else, a low ranking could still affect a candidate's political fate.[19]

To begin, the Index ought to matter when the party heuristic is unavailable—during the primary, when candidates compete against members of their own party, or during the general election in a nonpartisan race. In these low-information races, voters don't have a party label to sort candidates, so any means of distinguishing one candidate from another is potentially important. Indeed, not only should the Index itself provide a heuristic for voters, but it should also affect which organizations and newspapers endorse the candidate, thus influencing another basis on which voters cast their ballots.

Further, even in races where the party heuristic matters, the Index may affect the behind-the-scenes maneuvering that determines which candidates get put forward. Party elites play an important role in selecting the candidates who eventually run. During this "invisible primary,"[20] their decisions about funding and endorsements can determine who ends up running and winning the party primary. Imagine that you were a party leader, major donor, or get-out-the-vote organizer. There are a large number of candidates competing for your support. Why would you back someone whose ranking has rendered him potentially damaged goods? And wouldn't a high ranking increase a candidate's standing in your eyes? Even if the ranking will matter only rarely, a risk-averse political operative will prefer to place a bet on someone without any handicaps. These behind-the-scenes decisions all matter to a candidate's political fate, and they all increase the likelihood that politicians will care about how their state or locality ranks on the Index.

Deflection? A skeptic might also worry that a Democracy Index cannot temper existing political incentives because it is too easy to deflect politically.[21] Deflection is, of course, a routine move in political debate. One might imagine, for instance, a secretary of state arguing that it's not her fault that the state ranks poorly because the legislature hasn't granted her sufficient resources or local officials are at fault.

This claim, however, underestimates the power of rankings. Rankings work precisely because most citizens will not pay enough attention to move past the ranking itself. As I explain in the next chapter, even if voters actually paid enough attention to what was said during that ensuing debate, a useful conversation might emerge.

A more likely deflection strategy would be a claim of political bias. If the Democracy Index is put out by a group that voters easily identify as liberal or conservative, it is unlikely to get the right kind of traction. Voters need not look beyond the ranking for deflection to work; they just need to know who released the ranking to dismiss it. For all of their glories, the ACLU and the Cato Institute are not the right groups to put out the Index.*

Realigning local incentives. As noted in chapter 1, partisanship isn't the only reason our election system does not function as well as it should. Even when politics are working correctly—when politicians are attentive to what voters want—political incentives run against election reform. Local officials compete only on issues that voters can see. When a problem is invisible, a race to the bottom ensues.

A ranking system not only makes the problems in our election system *visible* to voters, but it casts those issues in explicitly competitive terms. By ranking states and localities against one another, the Democracy Index should help shame local officials into doing the right thing.

Consider, for instance, the competition that seems to have been spurred by one of the rare comparative metrics we have in election administration: the residual vote rate. In the wake of the 2000 election, reformers and political scientists used the residual vote rate as a rough proxy for assessing how many votes had been lost to machine problems, bad ballot design, and the like. As a Caltech/MIT study observes, when jurisdictions "were told they had high residual rates in 2000," many "worked to cut them to a fraction of what they were by 2002,"[22] even before Congress provided funding for new machines. Georgia, for example, had a high (3.2 percent) residual vote rate in 2000 but reduced it to 0.9 percent by 2002.[23] Reformers continue to rely on the residual vote rate to pressure localities to do better. A recent Brennan Center report, for instance, argues that residual vote rates should not be higher than 1 percent.[24]

We see a similar effect with other ranking systems. Take the Government Performance Project, a Pew Center on the States effort, which grades states based on their management practices.[25] The GPP was in large part the brainchild of Katherine Barrett and Richard Greene. This married couple used to write for major magazines, with Barrett focusing on public policy issues and Greene working on fiscal accountability in the private sector. Their jobs led to an unusual form of pillow talk: "Two spouses usually

*Similarly, it is essential that the Index's metrics appeal to all voters. If the ranking's opponents can point to a set of metrics reliably identified with one side of the partisan divide, the Index may lose its power.

don't talk about reforming public health systems in the Northeast," laughs Greene.[26] The more the two talked, the more they realized they were writing about a common question: management, particularly management in the public sector. The couple also began to notice that while "people always talk about [top officials'] politics and policies," there wasn't "a way to hold government accountable for how it managed itself." The GPP was designed to do just that.

The GPP has had a remarkable amount of success pushing states to do better on the management front. For instance, its emphasis "on the importance of workforce planning appeared to be central to enormous advances in the area," says Greene. While half of the states did such planning in 2005, forty-one did so by 2008.[27]

You can also see the GPP's effects on individual states. In Georgia, for instance, the governor made the state's midlevel ranking a central platform of change. The state began to measure itself against the GPP's criteria and has improved dramatically in a short time, moving itself from a B− to a B+ in three years.[28] Similarly, when the first GPP gave Alabama the lowest grade received by any state, state officials invited the GPP's architects to speak to its leadership and has been "getting steadily better" on many fronts, says Greene. Greene thinks Alabama's improvement is particularly impressive because success "is a moving target," as many of the states are improving at the same time.

Resting on one's laurels or keeping up with the Joneses? One might worry that even if the Democracy Index encourages states at the bottom of the list to improve, it won't create incentives for top-ranked states to do better. This situation would still represent an improvement on the status quo—at least the Index would provide an impetus for change *somewhere* in the system. But it is also possible that a ranking system will encourage top-ranked states to compete among themselves.

Consider, for instance, what took place when the first version of the Environmental Performance Index was released, showing Norway ranked second on the worldwide ranking.[29] As soon as the ranking was released, Norway invited Esty's team to visit. Members of the team expected to be greeted by press conferences and government ceremonies trumpeting Norway's extraordinary achievement. Instead, they were quietly ushered into closed-door sessions with top-level policymakers to discuss how Norway could improve its position. Norwegian leaders didn't care that they were ranked ahead of 120 other states. What mattered to them? *Finland* was number one.

As Esty has learned from administering the EPI, people don't expect every country to do equally well given wide disparities in resources. Peer groups are what matters for spurring healthy competition,[30] an observation confirmed by cutting-edge social science research.[31] The crisis the EPI ranking prompted in Belgium, for instance, occurred because it was ranked well below its European counterparts. Cameron Quinn, who served as the top elections officer under Virginia's Governor Jim Gilmore, confirms that election administrators look to peers for solutions. She says that when she needed help, she talked to her colleagues in North Carolina and Maryland, the states "aligned with Virginia."[32]

Given the salience of peer groups, we might expect that the jurisdictions most likely to be influenced by the Democracy Index are those that fall outside of where we might expect them to land given their resources or reputation or geography. People would take notice if a resource-rich states like Connecticut or New York fell low in the rankings or if one of the Midwestern states fell well below its neighbors. We might similarly expect the lowest-ranked states to care less about who is number one and more about who is at the bottom of the list. It's an idea nicely captured in the movie *Annapolis*, where the second-worst plebe in the outfit explains to the hero that Arkansas needs Mississippi to keep it from "being the worst state in the whole country." The plebe tells the hero, who's at the very bottom of the class, that he needs him to stay: "You're my Mississippi. . . . [I]f Mississippi quits, then all of a sudden Arkansas is the worst state in the whole country."[33] Even states in the middle of the ranking should be influenced by peer group rankings. As the Brennan Center's Justin Levitt notes, "Peer groups turn B students into D students"[34]—that is, those who don't improve will drop in the rankings because we are using a different yardstick.

A skeptic might worry that local competition matters only for issues that are important enough for people to "vote with their feet," like schools and taxes.[35] If someone at a cocktail party told you she was going to move to a different state in order to find better polling places or an easier registration system, you'd probably decide it's time for a refill.

It is a mistake, however, to assume that people must vote with their feet before local officials will pay attention. Politicians pay attention to issues even when they have what academics would call "a captive constituency."

They do so for a simple reason. They are risk averse and would rather represent happy constituents. Local officials worry not only about latent crises that might develop, but the cumulative effect of one bad headline after another. They also like to tout their successes, which is why one often sees high rankings proudly announced on local and state websites.

The worry about captive constituencies is nonetheless well taken. It reminds us to recognize the limits of any strategy designed to generate a "race to the top" in election reform. There are lots of issues competing for voters' attention, and a ranking system is not going to push election reform ahead of bread-and-butter issues like jobs and the economy. States will continue to feel pressure to commit resources to the many other problems they face. What the Democracy Index does is give election reform a much-needed boost in this competition for resources. And that is a good deal better than nothing.

Do People Care Enough about Election Reform for an Index to Work?

The arguments above depend on a crucial assumption: that some voters will care about election administration some of the time. We already have most of the raw ingredients for a successful movement: a superficially popular issue, a rough consensus that there's a problem, an engaged reform community, and semiregular crises to place the issue on the legislative agenda. The question is whether voters will get engaged enough to reverse the political incentives that run against change.

A skeptic might argue that voters will never care enough about reform to pay attention to a ranking. After all, the *U.S. News and World Report* ranking is read by so many people because anyone with a kid applying to college has a personal stake in the question. But our relationship to election administration is more tenuous and less personal.

Although we can't know for sure whether a Democracy Index would have an effect on voters, it would be a mistake to infer that voter preferences are fixed. We are dealing with what political scientists call an endogeneity problem. Voter opinions tend to be quite fluid. They are shaped by institutions, the media, and political elites. Political scientists E. E. Schattschneider argued that the ability to define a problem and its solution "is the supreme instrument of power,"[36] an idea buttressed by a long-standing political science literature on the importance of "framing."[37] The endogeneity problem makes it hard to figure out whether the Democracy Index will be enough to change voter preferences. In thinking about this question, however, we must think in dynamic terms.

There are several reasons to be optimistic about the Index's potential. First, other indices have made a splash even though they don't involve issues that affect people as directly as the quality of their children's education. The Environmental Performance Index, for instance, had an effect on environmental policy well before global warming became a household word and everyone began to fancy himself an environmentalist. And the Government Performance Project's evaluation of state management systems—a topic that surely ranks above election reform on the boredom scale—generates hundreds of news stories whenever it is released. Unless reporters and politicians have a tin ear, that's a sign that something is afoot.

Second, reformers *have* been able to get traction on election issues when they can frame them effectively. As Jonah Goldman points out, debates about paper trails have become salient in large part because reformers came up with a simple metaphor for capturing the problem: if we can get a receipt from an ATM, why can't touch-screen vote machines generate a paper trail?[38] That frame drives some experts crazy because they think it fundamentally mischaracterizes the problem.[39] But it's certainly driven policymaking,[40] confirming physicist G. C. Lichtenberg's observation that "a good metaphor is something even the police should keep an eye on." If the Index can provide a similarly intuitive frame for the public, it too ought to get traction with voters. At the very least, there are enough stories on election administration controversies these days that a Democracy Index would surely generate some press, even if it were only a sidebar to ongoing reporting.

Finally and most importantly, the key difference between the Democracy Index and many other indices is that the Democracy Index has a ready-made ally that cares deeply about this information: political parties. As is clear from the preceding discussion, political parties can use the Index for partisan advantage if they get the word out. Partisan politics—the engine that drives most public debates[41]—offers a built-in publicity machine for the Democracy Index.

The problem for election reformers in the past is that they have had a hard time harnessing political competition in the service of election reform. Though reform issues bubble up during an election crisis, for the most part politicians ignore them. Without political entrepreneurs to take up the cause, it is hard to get reform on the agenda. The fact that the Democracy Index turns election reform into a source of political advantage increases the likelihood that entrepreneurs will take up the cause. When politicians see a useful weapon, they are going to fire it.[42]

POLICYMAKERS AS LEVERAGE POINTS
Appealing to Politicians' Inner Wonk

The arguments above portray politicians in a rather bad light—as craven creatures motivated by self-interest. Political incentives plainly matter to elected officials, and it is important to be aware of them in thinking about the here-to-there problem. But the vast majority of elected officials try to do the right thing within existing political constraints. We therefore shouldn't underestimate the appeal of the right answer to politicians. And the appeal of the right answer is another reason that the Democracy Index should get the attention of the top-level officials who set policy and hold the purse strings. A performance index is something that appeals to every politician's inner wonk.

Giving politicians a baseline. In many ways, the Index serves the same purpose for top-level policymakers as it does for voters: it gives them a baseline for refereeing debates between the election administrators who work for them and the reformers who lobby them. Policymakers hear plenty of untrustworthy arguments from administrators who aren't doing their job properly. And they grow pretty tired of the insistent drumbeat for change emanating from reformers. Top-level policymakers face the same dilemma that the Supreme Court justices did in the voter ID case. They have to pick sides, and they need a guide to do so.

While top policymakers may be reluctant to hold election officials accountable based on the necessarily atmospheric opinions of reformers, they are likely to be convinced by hard numbers and comparative data. Election administrators can talk all they want about what they have done. But they cannot get around the stark reality of a ranking: Is the system working or not? And why is the state next door doing so much better?

Consider, for example, the success that election reformers have had with the Election Incident Reporting System (EIRS),[43] a web-based system that allows voter protection groups and individuals to report problems they've encountered in the last few elections. As Charles Stewart of MIT explains, the results of the EIRS are "suggestive at best"[44] because they depend on reporting rather than random sampling, the gold standard of social science research.

Nonetheless, the EIRS data have become an important tool for reformers.[45] That is because the data are available at the state and county level, allowing reformers to tell state legislators and local council members that problems exist in *their* neighborhoods. If the EIRS, despite its flaws, has helped reformers make headway in reform debates, imagine what a more rigorous yardstick could do to smooth the path for reform.

Identifying policy priorities. Rankings also attract the attention of top-level officials because they flag policymaking priorities. Legislators and governors are often bombarded with information. They hear lots of complaints, listen to lots of requests for funding, and sift through lots of reports. What they need is something that helps them separate the genuine problems from run-of-the-mill complaints, a means of distinguishing the signal from the static. A ranking can perform that role, as it focuses on systemic problems and provides a realistic baseline for judging performance.

Consider, for instance, what occurred in Mexico when the first version of the Environmental Performance Index (then called the Environmental Sustainability Index) was released.[46] Environmentalists had spent a lot of time trying to convince Mexico it had a problem. They ended up spending most of their time addressing low-level bureaucrats. When the first version of the EPI came out, ranking Mexico in the bottom fifth of the countries evaluated, it caught the attention of Mexico's president. Dan Esty's team received dozens of calls and emails from Mexican officials up and down the political hierarchy, all complaining about Mexico's ranking and, eventually, trying to figure out how to fix it. Mexican bureaucrats cared because the president cared.

ELECTION ADMINISTRATORS AS LEVERAGE POINTS

Building Alliances and Encouraging Self-Policing

A final, and often underappreciated, leverage point for reform is election administrators—the people who do the day-to-day work of running our election system. We usually assume that pressure for change can only come from the outside—from voters or reformers or top-level policymakers. But some of the most effective lobbyists for change are people working inside the system. Moreover, the long-term health of any administrative agency depends heavily on bureaucrats' policing themselves through professional norms. The Democracy Index would help on both fronts. It gives election administrators the information they need to lobby for much-needed resources. At the same time, the Index has the potential to promote stronger professional norms within the field.

Arming existing allies. The Democracy Index would be useful in arming existing allies, giving administrators already sympathetic to reform the information they need to make the case for change. The Index should be especially helpful in lobbying for resources. As one political scientist told me, "The people really to blame [for election problems] are the legislators and county commissioners," who have starved election administrators of resources. The Democracy Index, he says, is just what local administrators need to "beat the crap out of them."[47]

Lynn Olson of Quality Counts, a system that grades states based on their educational policies, confirms how useful rankings can be for bureaucrats. A bad ranking provides a justification for getting more resources; a good ranking helps them protect a policy that is under attack.[48] Philip Joyce—a longtime leader in the Government Performance Project—agrees. For instance, he notes that after Alabama received a lackluster C− from the GPP, state administrators used the report to build support for the governor's reform plans.[49] Ranking systems have already served a useful purpose in the elections context. For instance, Kentucky secretary of state Trey Grayson used a ranking that showed Kentucky lagging behind on campaign finance reform to push for a new bill.[50]

Generating more alliances. The Democracy Index might do more than help sympathetic bureaucrats lobby for reform from the inside; it might also create *more* allies within the system. There has been a long and not so merry war between election reformers and administrators. The word *poisonous* is often used to describe it. Needless to say, tense relations between reformers and administrators are an obstacle to change. As Edward Hailes of the Advancement Project observes, it is much better for reformers "to get inside election administrators' heads than in their faces."[51]

While reformers and bureaucrats in other arenas don't always get along, relations seem particularly strained in the elections context, a problem that may be partially traceable to the absence of data. That's because the absence of data makes it possible for one side to be obdurate and the other to engage in occasional histrionics. It's like the policymaking version of *The Odd Couple.*

Election administrators play Oscar Madison's role. They preside over a messy, chaotic system. In a world without data, it can be easier for an administrator to deny that a problem exists than buckle down to fix it. Put yourselves in the shoes of the Joy Streaters of the world, struggling to do a big job with few resources. Is it surprising that change seems like a pain, and the people needling you to change seem like a bigger pain? Surely we can forgive election administrators' bristling at the "holier-than-thou-ness" sometimes displayed by reformers. Election administrators are the one group that does a harder job and makes less money than reformers. The temptation is to shut reformers out instead of turning to them for help. It's no wonder that election administrators sometimes come off as grumpy, gruff, and cynical.

Reformers, in turn, sometimes play the role of the histrionic Felix Unger (minus the suit). The absence of data may lead reformers to up the rhetorical ante in reform debates. Without concrete data on performance, it is very hard to get policymakers' attention. So reformers are tempted to overstate the problem or present solutions as silver bullets.[52] Fearing that any concession will license election administrators to ignore real problems (the old worry about "giving 'em an inch"), reformers sometimes speak as if a single discarded ballot or a single voter deterred is one too many.

The truth is that there are trade-offs involved in designing any election system, something that comparative performance data would reveal.

Guaranteeing a precise ballot count may delay election results. Making it easy for members of one group to cast a ballot may make it harder for those in another. An easier registration system may make the balloting process more chaotic. Moreover, as with every reform project, there is always a point of diminishing returns. Sometimes localities *ought* to be investing in cops and teachers rather than spending large amounts of money to make marginal improvements to their voting systems. In a world without data, the risk is that election reformers appear unduly fastidious and reinforce election administrators' sense that their demands are excessive and their claims are oversold.

Election administrators and reformers should not be playing to these stereotypes. They are serious people doing serious work, and they need each other to get the job done. A Democracy Index might provide a disciplining device, improving arguments on both sides. Reformers won't need to resort to heavy-handed rhetoric to make their case, and it will be harder for election administrators to deny they have a problem. But data will also force reformers to choose their fights wisely, giving election administrators grounds for pushing back when a costly reform seems unlikely to produce results.

As to the not so merry war, my own guess is that the absence of data is especially damaging to election administrators. That's a counterintuitive claim, as most people think that election administrators' incentives run the other way. But the absence of data, combined with the episodic way that we learn about problems, poses a devastating risk for election administrators. In a world without data, voters learn about problems only when there is a crisis, and they lack a comparative baseline for assessing what's going on. When an election fiasco occurs, voters tend to leap to the conclusion that the problem was deliberately engineered. After all, elections are a virtual black box. Voters know only that there's a crisis, that other places aren't experiencing the same problem, and that the person in charge has a partisan affiliation. It is all too easy to connect the dots.

Having learned a great deal from the Joy Streaters and Gary Smiths of the world, my assumption is that most election problems are caused by a resource shortage, not partisanship. There is a rule often invoked by computer programmers called "Hanlon's razor" which says that one should never attribute something to malice that can be adequately explained by stupidity. I wish we would adopt a similar rule in the elections arena: never attribute to partisanship that which can be adequately explained by deferred maintenance.

Take Matt Damschroder, former director of the Franklin County Board of Elections in Columbus, Ohio. In 2004, Franklin County had too few machines to deal with the extraordinarily high turnout for that race. People waited in line for as long as five or six hours to vote, and many voters left in frustration before they cast their ballots. Damschroder's own mother waited two hours in line, "and I still hear about it," he observes wryly.

I offer this controversial example quite deliberately, because the story of Franklin County is as close to *Rashomon* as an election controversy can get. Some use the phrase *Franklin County* as an epithet and cast Matt Damschroder as the story's chief villain. In the wake of the election, allegations flew that Franklin County had deliberately failed to put enough voting machines in its polling places. People also accused the elections board of allocating voting machines in a discriminatory fashion, putting fewer in precincts dominated by racial minorities and Democrats in order to deter them from voting.

Others tell a story about Franklin County that will be familiar by now—the story of deferred maintenance. While Monday morning quarterbacks think that the Franklin County elections board could have done better, particularly in distributing machines among polling places, they refuse to accept the Damschroder-as-Ohio's-Karl-Rove story. Damschroder, after all, is well respected by experts and has made a name for himself in Ohio as a straight shooter. He was well known for "criticiz[ing] and sometimes def[ying]" the policies of fellow Republican Kenneth Blackwell because they would "hinder voter registration."[53] Moreover, Franklin County's Board of Elections was bipartisan. Indeed, William Anthony, a Democratic member and then-chair of the board, was prominently quoted in the papers as saying, "I am a black man. Why would I sit there and disenfranchise voters in my own community? . . . I've fought my whole life for people's right to vote."[54]

Moreover, as Damschroder's supporters point out, it shouldn't be surprising that Franklin County didn't have enough machines, or that its board didn't do a great job planning for the election. During the prior two years, the Franklin County commissioners had granted the elections board only half of the funding it had requested to prepare for the 2004 election.[55] The county commissioners did what any self-interested politicians would do—funded the problems that were visible to their constituents. Want to guess which departments received full funding those years? Children's Services and the Sheriff's Office.

So what happened in Franklin County? Partisan mischief or deferred maintenance? The point here is not to resolve this debate. The point is that we *can't* resolve this debate. Our inability to get a firm read even on a highly publicized brouhaha like this one is something that should worry everyone. It should worry voters and policymakers because we don't know whether we are holding someone accountable or savaging an innocent person's reputation. And it should especially worry election administrators, because none of them wants to be the next Matt Damschroder.

A Democracy Index might help change this unfortunate dynamic. It would make systemic problems like deferred maintenance visible to voters and policymakers. It would help us distinguish between partisan shenanigans and the ailments that afflict most jurisdictions—a lack of professional expertise, poorly trained poll workers, too few resources. It would ensure that we reward the many election administrators doing a good job despite intense resource handicaps. And perhaps it could provide a partial antidote to the "poison" that has seeped into reform debates.

Helping Election Administrators Police Themselves

Perhaps the most important role an Index could play with election administrators is to help create a consensus on best practices. When we think about improving a system, we generally assume that the pressure for reform comes from the outside. But the long-term health of any system depends on administrators policing themselves based on shared professional norms. Indeed, professional norms may ultimately be more important to a well-run system than pressures from the outside.

Why Professional Norms Matter

Professional norms are what my colleague Jerry Mashaw calls "soft law"[56] because they rely on an informal source of power—peer pressure. They work because government workers are just like the rest of us. They care what other people think, and they are likely to care most about the opinions of people in their own professional tribe.

Anyone who lives with a teenager—in fact, anyone who has *been* a teenager—knows that peer pressure can affect people's behavior. Social scientists have done extensive work identifying the ways in which the pressure to conform affects individual behavior.[57] Although peer pressure is responsible for some ridiculous things—Chia pets, tongue rings, the sartorial choices of the 1970s—it can serve useful ends in policymaking. Many professional groups—lawyers, accountants, engineers—possess shared norms about best practices. While these norms are often informal, they cabin the range of acceptable behavior. When professional identity becomes intertwined with particular practices, people's own sense that they are doing a good job depends on conforming to these norms. For those of us trying to suppress memories of high school, it's nice to know that the herd instinct can do a bit of good in the world.

It's not just peer pressure that causes people to conform to professional standards; it's also time constraints. No one has the time to think through the practical and moral considerations involved in every decision. Like voters, administrators need shorthand to guide their behavior. A professional consensus on best practices can represent a sensible heuristic for figuring out the right choice.

Peer pressure not only can shape individual behavior, but can push *institutions* to adopt reforms that experts have christened as best practices. Social science research on the "global polity"[58] reveals that despite vast cultural and resource differences among nation-states, countries follow what social scientist calls "common models or scripts of what a nation-state ought to be."[59] Mimicry even happens in areas where you'd think that cultural or economic differences would trump. For instance, landlocked nations seem to follow global standards when designing their militaries, leaving them with navies without ports.[60] Countries where "scientists and engineers comprise less than 0.2 percent of the population, and research and development spending is infinitesimal," create science policy review boards to issue ethics reports and give guidance to scientists.[61]

We similarly see a great deal of imitation by state and local governments in the United States—instances where the adoption of a policy by a handful of institutions pushes others to adopt the same policy. At least since the late 1960s,[62] social scientists have documented the ways in which policies spread from state to state.[63] As one of the most recent and comprehensive studies explains, policy ideas of all sorts—from the adoption of city council–manager systems to crime control policies—can spread rapidly from "city to city [and] from state to state."[64]

Institutions imitate each other for roughly the same reasons that individuals do. Sociologists and anthropologists tend to emphasize peer pressure and social meaning—the ways in which behavioral "scripts" signal prestige and become the model for institutional behavior. Political scientists, in contrast, tend to emphasize the ways in which time pressures lead officials to use the decisions of others—particularly their peers—as a heuristic to guide their behavior.[65] Legislators in New York and Pennsylvania, for instance, might ask "WWJD?"—"What would Jersey do?"

The absence of professional norms in election administration. Unfortunately, professional norms that could shape individual and institutional behavior are largely absent in the elections arena, as are the vehicles for creating and spreading them. There is no accreditation system or training program used by election administrators across the country, nor is there a widely read trade magazine in the field. Although there are membership groups, most are locally oriented and do not have a sufficient membership to generate a fieldwide consensus.[66] These groups also do not provide as much support and service as other local government organizations, like the National Association of Counties or the National Conference of State Legislatures.[67]

Most importantly, the members of these associations are often reluctant to endorse best practices. For instance, one of the few nationwide groups in the field, the National Association of Secretaries of State, uses the term *shared* practices on the ground that local variation prevents the association from identifying which practice is best.[68] Similarly, Ray Martinez, a former commissioner of the Election Assistance Commission, the federal agency charged with issues of election administration, notes that whenever the EAC even raises the possibility of promoting best practices, it receives "pushback."[69] One political scientist bemoaned the field's resistance to best practices. "Every time I go to a conference, people tell me, 'That won't work where I'm from,' as if they lived on a different planet."[70]

The institution that seems to have made the most headway in promoting professional norms is the Election Center, a Texas-based nonprofit headed up by Doug Lewis. The Election Center offers training and continuing education to election administrators while serving as an advocate for their interests. Gary Smith, who heads up elections in Forsyth County, Georgia, felt so despondent about improving the system that he considered quitting, but then someone suggested he attend an Election Center conference. It "changed how I felt about elections,"[71] he told me—a high compliment from someone not prone to exaggerate. Unfortunately, the Election Center isn't yet big enough to reach most election administrators.

Can the Democracy Index Help?

The Democracy Index might provide a useful start toward building professional norms and disseminating good policies. If we focus on the issues deemed salient to sociologists and anthropologists, the question is whether the Democracy Index could generate professional peer pressure among election administrators or disseminate a "script" as to what constitutes a well-run system.

It's easy to see how the Democracy Index would at least provide a focal point for election administrators' attention. Surely it would be hard for anyone to resist checking how his state or locality measured up on the ranking. Administrators would want to peek at the Index for the same reason that people "Google" their own names or give a book a "Washington read" (scanning the Index to see what was said about them). If the Index were well designed and put out by a credible group, there is good reason to think that one's professional prestige would be increased by a high ranking, something that would be quite useful in a world where individuals and rulemaking bodies tend to mimic high-status people and institutions.[72] The Index might develop into a professional touchstone for the field.

In addition to generating professional peer pressure, the Democracy Index could help disseminate best practices. As election administrators and political scientists work through the data, they should be able to identify what policies succeed and thus help create scripts for a well-run system.

Consider, for example, the role that the GPP has played in generating and disseminating best practices among government administrators. Why do state administrators pay attention to the GPP? Philip Joyce, one of its architects, argues that the GPP is so effective because it is published by

Governing, a trade publication widely read and widely respected by state administrators.[73] State administrators care about the GPP report even though *Governing* is read mostly by other state administrators. It may not affect an administrator's political standing, but it matters to her professional standing.

Someone might worry that, consistent with the view of the National Association of Secretaries of State, there is too much local variation for a set of best practices to emerge within the field of election administration. I am frankly skeptical about that claim, at least when it is cast in broad terms. It is hard to imagine that we will not be able to identify some broad policies—funding, training policies, registration systems—that would be useful across jurisdictions.

I had a conversation about this with South Dakota's level-headed secretary of state, Chris Nelson. Like many people in the field, Nelson insists that local variation precludes the development of best practices and offered me trenchant examples of federal regulations that were ill-suited to his state's demographics. But he also told me about creating an electronic voter registration with the Department of Motor Vehicles that resulted in a thirteen-fold increase in registrations from one county alone.[74] That type of innovation seems like just the kind of idea that could be exported to other states. For this reason, I think Ohio's secretary of state, Jennifer Brunner, gets it right when she attributes the absence of a consensus on best practices to the dearth of data. Election administrators, she says, are "understaffed, overworked, [and] have often not documented their procedures," so how could best practices develop? Brunner is accordingly creating a state clearinghouse to collect and disseminate them.[75]

Even if it *is* impossible to create a consensus on model policy inputs, it should still be possible to generate professional norms about performance *outputs*. The Democracy Index could create something akin to a lingua franca in the realm of election administration, shared performance standards that would apply to localities regardless of their practices. For instance, a professional norm might deem that voting machines should not produce a residual vote rate higher than 1 percent. The Index might similarly generate performance baselines regarding the number of errors in the registration process or the number of poll worker complaints that fall within an acceptable range for a well-run system.

If we focus on the political science work on policy diffusion, we can similarly identify ways in which the Democracy Index might promote best practices among election administrators and institutions. Political scientists think that policy diffusion is most likely to occur when innovations in other states are visible. That's because policymakers tend to rely on information that is "timely, available, and salient."[76] One of the reasons that professional associations,[77] "policy entrepreneurs,"[78] and public interest groups or think tanks[79] matter, says Professor Andrew Karch, is that they "typically provide timelier, more accessible, and more detailed information about policy innovations" than other sources of information.[80]

The Democracy Index could be useful in this regard, because it can help policymakers to identify the innovation needle in a haystack of widely varying practices. It's just the kind of "information shortcut" that scholars like Karch argue policymakers need. The Index would give us a pretty good sense about which states and localities have performed best, and, if it is properly designed, should simultaneously offer information about which policy inputs drove that success. If, as Karch argues, "the most influential causal mechanisms" of the agenda-setting process are "those that can heighten the visibility of a policy innovation,"[81] the Index moves at least one step in the right direction.

Second, the Democracy Index might provide an opportunity to create a poor man's substitute for a vibrant professional network. Imagine, for instance, that the Democracy Index website provided not just the rankings and the underlying performance data, but tables and charts within each category identifying which jurisdictions followed which policies. The website might also provide links to extant research on the subject, even examples of implementing legislation and contact information for jurisdictions that have implemented the policy successfully. The Index would thus provide a portal that not only identifies which policies are succeeding, but gives policymakers instant access to the best available information on how to implement them. Here again, if the problem for officials is how "to sift through the massive amount of information that is available to find what is needed,"[82] perhaps a well-designed DemocracyIndex.com site could play a useful role.

There's limited evidence that rankings can promote this type of contact and information sharing between jurisdictions. For instance, Richard

Greene, senior consultant to the Government Performance Project, says that states that earn a good grade on the GPP are regularly contacted by other states for more information about their policies. In Greene's words, "States are absolutely hungry for good, solid, well-researched information to help them do what they do better."[83]

The Democracy Index is not a perfect substitute for the many mechanisms that social scientists have identified for creating professional norms and diffusing policy innovations—far from it. But a ranking system does have the potential to move us in the right direction.

CONCLUSION

If we want to get from "here to there" in election reform, a Democracy Index would help reformers target the three main leverage points in the reform process: voters, top policymakers, and election administrators. A ranking can provide a useful shorthand for voters and top policymakers, helping them hold election officials accountable for their missteps. By making election problems visible, it also has the potential to harness the twin engines of partisanship and local competition in the service of reform. While the Democracy Index won't shame every politician into doing better, it should hang like the sword of Damocles over the political ambitions of partisan and local officials. It should thus soften parts of the terrain on which reform battles are fought.

Even if the Index fails on the political front, it should nonetheless help election administrators make the case for change and develop the professional norms that are crucial to a well-functioning system. By providing a professional touchstone and making successful policies visible to election administrators and policymakers, the Index should help push in the direction of more professional management and better policies.

4 Is the Game Worth the Candle?

In the prior chapters, I identified the many reasons to think that a Democracy Index could help us get from here to there in election reform. In this chapter I focus on the other side of the cost-benefit equation, examining the problems associated with ranking and strategies to mitigate them. Rankings create at least four kinds of problems:

- People imbue them with an objectivity they don't deserve.
- They can target the wrong people.
- They may induce institutions to compete along the wrong dimensions.
- They create an incentive to cheat.

The first two problems are the natural consequences of distillation. Ranking requires a trade-off between precision and accessibility, and there are costs associated with this trade-off no matter what choice you make. The second two issues are what you might call "happiness problems"; they occur if the Index starts to get traction, but they can undermine its success in the long term. Below, I discuss each in turn and offer my own take on how the costs and benefits play out.

THE TRADE-OFF BETWEEN PRECISION AND ACCESSIBILITY

Rankings simplify. It is an inevitable consequence of trying "to provide *one* answer to a question when that answer depends on several bits of data," in the words of Oxford's Stein Ringen.[1] Distilling information can serve many useful ends, but any effort to rank necessarily involves a trade-off between precision and accessibility, or "rigor and intuition," to use Dan Esty's phrase.[2]

This trade-off pops up in just about every policymaking debate, not just when we talk about rankings. Just think about the title of this book. Because my proposed ranking measures the performance of an election system, it is more accurately termed a "Democratic Performance Index" or even an "Election Administration Performance Index."[3] So what is the right choice? Pick the most accurate title, even if it sounds technical and dry? Or choose a name that voters will remember?

It is a mistake, however, to insist that rankings necessarily *over*simplify, as if any type of shorthand is necessarily illegitimate in policymaking. Policymaking would be impossible without shorthand. If all shorthand were eliminated, we wouldn't have a GDP and thus couldn't distinguish between an economic blip and a recession. Congress would never stop holding hearings, because there would always be more testimony to collect. *Consumer Reports* would go out of business. Lord knows what the New York Stock Exchange would do.

Even *disaggregated* data are a form of shorthand. As Dan Esty notes, "Quantification is about distillation."[4] The raw ingredients of the Democracy Index are stand-ins for a vast and complicated process that no individual could possibly evaluate firsthand. The very purpose of data is to distinguish between what Esty calls "signal" and "noise."[5] Consider, for instance, Roger Angell's evocative description of baseball box scores:

> A box score is more than a capsule archive. It is a precisely etched miniature of the sport itself. . . . [that] permits the baseball fan, aided by experience and memory, to extract from a box score the same joy, the same hallucinatory reality, that prickles the scalp of a musician when he glances at a score of Don Giovanni and actually hears bassos and sopranos, woodwinds and violins.[6]

Because shorthand is inevitable, the real question is what kind of shorthand to use. In the prior chapters, I've offered a lot of reasons to favor ranking as a form of shorthand. But there are costs that accompany those benefits. The first is that voters will imbue the results with greater precision and accuracy than they deserve. The second is that a ranking may provide such a blunt tool for holding people accountable that it ends up putting pressure on the wrong people.

No Ranking Is Objective

You might worry about rankings because people think they are precise and objective when they aren't. Attaching a number to an assessment lends it an aura of absolute truth. People are sure that the institution ranked first is better than the one ranked second, and they think that a ranking conveys meaningful information about the distance between, say, first and second or thirty-fourth and thirty-fifth. Indexes suggest not only precision, but another quality associated with mathematics: objectivity. Perhaps our affection for ranking stems from the fact that we were all once muddled adolescents, longing for answers in a place where only the football coaches and math teachers were certain about anything.

Needless to say, the reality is quite different from the perception. Ranking requires a large number of discretionary (and thus debatable) choices. Every stop along the way—deciding what to measure, how to measure it, and how to add the measurements together—requires a normative judgment.

David Roodman, chief architect of the Commitment to Development Index, is well aware of these trade-offs. Roodman's unusual background in math and communications gives him an acute sense of ranking's theoretical shortcomings and its practical utility as a "communications vehicle."[7] The challenge involved in ranking, he jokes, is "to do something that is analytically impossible in a way that is analytically credible."[8]

The most debatable aspect of ranking. Just to ground the analysis a bit, let me focus on what's likely to be the most debatable choice for any ranking: how to weight the data. Even when most people can agree on what to measure and how to measure it, there will be considerable disagreement about how to aggregate the data into a single ranking.

The trade-off between precision and accessibility is particular acute in this context because the most sophisticated weighting techniques are likely to be the least transparent. The easiest, most transparent strategy is to pick commonsense categories and average the scores assigned to each category, just as one would calculate a grade point average. I propose just such a strategy for the Democracy Index. Needless to say, there will be other ways to aggregate the data (after all, what are the odds that everything is equally important?). Or take the mini-index I offered in chapter 2, which ranks states based on how much data they disclosed to the Election Assistance Commission. When I got to the weighting question, I favored transparency over methodological sophistication and thus weighted each category equally. The idea that the thirteen categories designated by the EAC are equally important is, needless to say, debatable.

Why would one choose an equal weighting strategy, as I did and as many index designers have done? The reason is simple: other weighting strategies are just as debatable and a good deal less transparent. As Ringen observes, "If the weights are not objectively known . . . go[ing] by the simplest assumption" is a sensible choice.[9]

While I think the decision to weight categories equally is defensible, no one would suggest that there is an easy way to resolve these debates, save perhaps the clueless husband in the *New Yorker* cartoon who asks his wife, "You want a child, I want a dog. Can't we compromise?"[10] As a practical matter, the only way to settle these debates is to settle them.

Still, I don't want to overstate the costs of simplification here. As Richard Greene of the GPP observes, "It's okay for people to debate" the choices made, as long as "no one thinks they are foolish."[11] Stein Ringen offers the most cogent argument for ranking. "We *always* rely on conventions of some kind or other in any effort at measurement, and indexing is in that respect not extraordinary," he writes. "As long as we use sensible conventions and explain the procedures, there is nothing unscientific in it."[12]

Dan Esty would surely agree. The designers of the EPI, after consulting numerous experts, chose to divide the environmental performance metrics they were using into two main categories—measures of environmental health (which includes things like child mortality rates, drinking water quality, sanitation) and measures of ecosystem vitality (which includes things like timber harvest rates, overfishing, and renewable energy).[13] Remarkably, although this fifty-fifty weighting is in theory the most contestable part of the EPI, in practice it's been the least contested.[14] Esty attributes that fact to two things. The fifty-fifty breakdown is intuitive. And no one has come up with a better strategy.

Similarly, David Roodman, the chief architect of the Commitment to Development Index, argues that in the absence of a consensus on weighting, an equal weighting strategy represents the simplest and most transparent method for assembling the CDI. Roodman told me that months of consulting with academic experts convinced him that his simple weighting strategy was the right one. Why? No one else had a suggestion that could garner a consensus. For every category, there was always one expert or another suggesting it was entitled to more weight than it got.[15] For this reason, Roodman chose the most transparent one. "Weighting things equally," he says, "says that I don't know the answer."[16]

Mitigating Strategies

The costs associated with ranking are inevitable, but they can be mitigated by choices the Index's architects make in designing and publicizing the ranking.

Don't oversell. In order to reduce the costs associated with ranking, designers of the Index must also be careful about overselling its objectivity or accuracy. It's tough to exercise restraint. Including caveats in every sentence is a surefire recipe for rhetorical constipation. Remember that I opened this book by noting that the dearth of data made it difficult to be confident in any claims about our election system. Just think about how long this book would be if I began every sentence with "The best evidence available suggests that . . ." But even a well-designed Index can offer only a rough sense of how states and localities are doing based on reasonable but nonetheless debatable choices. The Index won't allow us to draw fine-grained distinctions. The difference between first and second—or even first and sixth—may be illusory.

The designers of the Index should thus acknowledge those limitations early and often. Problems in the data should be discussed forthrightly. The designers of the Index should note its lack of precision. They should also identify—and explain—the judgment calls they made along the way. Brochures and websites that accompany the Index should clearly explain the normative and methodological choices that were made in assembling the it. All of the data should be publicly available, and the mechanism for aggregating the data should be transparent.

Ideally, the materials accompanying the Index should not only make the designers' choices clear, but show how those choices affected the ranking themselves. One way to do that is to show how a different choice would affect the rankings. Take, for instance, the disclosure index I offered in chapter 2. As close readers might notice, there's a note indicating that Hawaii may have been unfairly handicapped because much of its underreporting was due to a quarantined leper colony with a population of 147 people. Should I have eliminated that county from the ranking because—to use a phrase I never expected to pen—"Come on, it's a quarantined leper colony of 147 people!"? Should I have kept the county in, on the theory that there are other places with reporting handicaps? Given that both choices seemed reasonable, the best solution seemed to be to go ahead with the ranking but show precisely how that judgment affected Hawaii's standing and where Hawaii would rank were the quarantined county excluded.

Alternatively, designers of the Index could show how their judgments influenced the rankings by allowing people to rerun the rankings themselves using their own criteria[17]—the election geek's version of "choose your own adventure." It is likely, for instance, that the relative weight given to different components of the Index will matter a good deal to the results. Designers of the Index might therefore create a website that asks someone to identify which issues matter to him and how he evaluates their relative importance. The website would then calculate a new state-by-state ranking based on the choices the person has made.

One might worry that every low-ranked jurisdiction will immediately try to rejigger the rankings to improve its standing. The designers of the Democracy Index ought to welcome such efforts. Some jurisdictions will improve their standing only if they make implausible choices, something that reform groups will be quick to point out. Some jurisdictions may find an equally sensible ranking system that raises their standing, perhaps even revealing problems in the Index along the way. Given that one of the main purposes of the Index is to start a more productive conversation about election reform, this is all to the good. The conversation about election administration will improve, and the Index may improve along with it.

Reevaluate constantly. Another important strategy for a successful Democracy Index is constant reevaluation. People who create indexes introduce prototypes and updates for the same reason that software engineers release beta versions of their programs: to work out the bugs. The Democracy Index 1.0 is likely to be quite different from subsequent iterations.[18] Before, during, and after each version of the Index is released, it will be crucial to get feedback on the ranking and the judgments that go into it.

In this respect, designers of the Index should think like academics. The best scholars are those who hear serious criticisms of their work . . . and are thrilled by it. They want criticism to come in the same form as good whiskey—straight up. So, too, the architects of the Index should put the prototype—and every iteration thereafter—in front of a "murderers' row" of its toughest critics. Designers of the Index should similarly welcome criticism from the people being evaluated. Dan Esty argues that "angry jurisdictions are good"[19] because they are going to help you make your index better. Moreover, as David Roodman points out, if the goal of the Index is to raise awareness about a problem, "An attack on an index is a victory."[20]

Evaluating the Tradeoff between Precision and Accessibility

While the mitigating strategies described above are useful, they cannot eliminate the costs associated with oversimplification. Even if the Index's architects rigorously adhere to the suggestions outlined above, voters are still likely to overestimate the objectivity and accuracy of the ranking. To return to the Gary Larson cartoon about what dogs hear, there is a danger that even when the Democracy Index is presented with caveats and cautious warnings, all that voters will hear is "——, ——, my state ranked forty-ninth, ——."

Indeed, the reasons the Democracy Index is likely to succeed are precisely the reasons that we are wary of indexes in the first place: voters may not look past the ranking itself. The costs associated with ranking are simply the flip side of its benefits: accessibility, simplicity, popular appeal. Given that we cannot make these problems go away, we ought to be clear-eyed about acknowledging them.

So how do we balance the benefits of accessibility against the costs of imprecision? While the concerns described in this section are serious, in my view the benefits still outweigh them. To begin, even if voters vest too much faith in an Index, at least they'll be putting their trust in what ought to be a pretty good measure of democratic performance. The fact that there isn't an objective answer on these issues doesn't mean that the Index's architects will have a license to engage in free-form democratic engineering. There *are* answers to these questions, and some answers will be better than others. If the Index is properly designed, even those who quibble with a decision should nonetheless think it was a reasonable one.

On the other side of the equation, there are costs associated with *not* having a ranking. We're back to the "As opposed to what?" question. A ranking will surely oversimplify the state of affairs. But, as Ringen observes, "While some information gets lost, something else is gained."[21] Reams of comparative data cannot give us a clear view of how jurisdictions are performing overall. As with party labels, rankings tell voters about the "big thing" even if they lose track of the "little things." A well-designed Index fares particularly well when it is compared to the other shorthand citizens use in evaluating voting processes—anecdote, haphazard evidence of a crisis, or partisan labels. The public places unwarranted faith in each of these heuristics. Each leads to oversimplification and mistake of a more significant sort than a well-designed Index will. And not one of them gets us any closer to improving our failing system. In this context, something seems better than nothing.*

The bottom line here depends almost entirely on what you think the Democracy Index is for.[22] If the goal is simply to convey information, the answer is obvious: don't rank. Presenting data in disaggregated form will almost always be better than ranking. But if the goal is to improve the policymaking process—to correct a failure in the political market—the only thing that beats a good ranking is a better one.

Targeting the Right People

There is another cost to a ranking like the Democracy Index: it can lead voters to target the wrong people. In earlier chapters, I've loosely lumped together the people who decide how our elections get administered. But the identity of these "deciders," to borrow one of George Bush's favorite terms, will vary from state to state, and these variations matter if we want

*None of this is to say that we will improve the political process by giving people bad information. As America's Manolo-shod philosopher, Carrie Bradshaw, once observed, at some point "the art of compromise become[es] compromising." Something is not always better than nothing. But a pretty good something usually is.

the Index to work. In some places, local officials play an important role in allocating money and setting rules. In other places, state officials matter most. Moreover, at both levels, control over elections is often divided. At the state level, it may be shared by a secretary of state and a legislature; at the local level, an elections board and county council may be in charge.

Decentralization poses a problem for the Democracy Index. The goal of the ranking is to put pressure on the right people. But the Index will sometimes be too blunt a tool to do so. It could end up placing pressure on officials who can't do much about what is happening on the ground. A single ranking tells us that "the state" or "the county" has a problem, but it does not tell us who within that jurisdiction is at fault.

Imagine, for instance, that the Democracy Index ranked a state forty-seventh in the nation, and voters began to pester its secretary of state. She might legitimately complain that the real problems with the system stem from decisions made at the local level. Or she might blame the legislature or vice versa. How do voters figure out who's at fault?

Mitigating Strategies

There are several things that designers of the Index could do to help ensure that the right people are held accountable when the Index is released. First, if the data permit, the Index should rank localities within the states, just as it ranks the states. An intrastate ranking would allow the media—and therefore perhaps voters—to identify where the biggest problems are. If most of the scores that depressed the state's ranking came from one or two counties, the secretary of state should be able to redirect the media's attention to local administrators. Alternatively, the intrastate comparison may reveal that the blame lies with the state. Comparative data on local performance, for instance, would reveal issues that might not be visible if we examine only state-level data. For example, many political scientists think that small and rural election systems are especially likely to be understaffed and underfunded. An intrastate ranking would help states identify that problem and fix it.

Similarly, by helping identify the drivers of performance, the Index could help the media target the right culprit. Imagine, for instance, that a low ranking spurred an "am not, are too" debate between the secretary of state and state legislators, each blaming the other for the state's low ranking.

If funding mattered most, the secretary of state could point her finger at the legislature and would have good evidence to feed reporters. If training poll workers was the key to success, the press would know to hound the secretary of state.

The Costs and Benefits of the Blame Game

Although the strategies noted above may reduce the likelihood that the Index will lead voters to target the wrong officials, they aren't foolproof. As noted in the previous chapter, people tend to pay attention to the numbers, not the nuances, when looking at rankings. The danger is that voters won't pay attention to the debate that ensues after the Index is released. That makes an Index a necessarily blunt and imperfect tool for holding people accountable.

The real issue, then, is whether we can live with this cost. If we return to the crucial question —"As opposed to what?"—a ranking system still seems superior to nothing. At present, pressure is rarely placed on *any* election official, so no one needs to bother with finger pointing. Bickering about *which* officials are doing their job seems like a better conversation to be having than no discussion at all.

Moreover, even if the Democracy Index cannot tell us precisely who is responsible for a state's low ranking, it creates an incentive for every election official to make the case that he, at least, is doing everything he should. While the Index may not resolve the debate in the eyes of voters, it should at least jump-start a conversation that we ought to be having. After all, you can't finger-point without endorsing a solution. These debates should help generate some new allies in the election system, or at least put some officials on the record as supporting change.

A litigator would probably tell you that there's no need to worry about any of this. Plaintiffs sometimes run into the same problem voters do: they know who is to blame generally for a problem but can't pinpoint the exact culprit. For instance, when a plaintiff isn't sure how to apportion blame for an injury among several defendants, it can cause a problem. If the case goes to trial, the defendants can spend all of their time denying that they are to blame, and the plaintiff may go home empty-handed through no fault of her own. Here's a hypothetical I always give my Civil Procedure class. Imagine that three companies dumped chemicals in the river, but the victim doesn't know which one caused the harm. For each company, there's only a 33 percent chance that it was the one that caused the injury. A jury might be 100 percent confident that *one* of the three defendants did the dirty deed, but it can't say that it was more likely than not that Company A (or B or C) was guilty.

Courts have come up with a smart solution to this problem: they hold all of the defendants "jointly and severally liable." That means that the victim can demand full payment from any one of defendants, and the defendant who pays can in turn demand that the other defendants pay their share. The court, in effect, tells the defendants responsible for the harm to play the blame game among themselves. In practice, the strategy usually leads the defendants to use their considerable resources to get the goods on each other, something that gets us much closer to the truth. "Joint and several liability" puts the defendants to work for the victim.

The Index is the policymaking equivalent of "joint and several liability" for election officials. If voters put pressure on a secretary of state for a poor ranking when the state legislature really deserves the blame, it becomes the job of the secretary of state—not the voters—to make the case against the legislature. While that may seem unfair, the truth is that the secretary of state has more information than voters do, and she is better situated to direct attention to the source of the problem than anyone else. "Joint and several liability" in politics puts election official to work for the voters.

The case for some version of joint and several liability is even stronger when voters hold state officials' feet to the fire for the missteps of local jurisdictions. At the end of the day, the states decide how much money and power localities have. State officials may squawk that it is unfair to punish them for mistakes made by local officials over whom they purportedly have no control. But the final responsibility for determining how much control local officials exercise lies with the state. If top state officials choose to maintain a decentralized system that isn't working, they should live with the consequences of that choice.

"Joint and several liability" may even work better here than in the litigation context. In a lawsuit, the defendants just fight with each other and go home. In the election context, placing local and state officials on the same hook might encourage them to cooperate more often. After all, they all have a stake in raising the state's ranking.

HAPPINESS PROBLEMS

In addition to the two problems noted above—both having to do with the trade-off between precision and accessibility—there are at least two other potential pitfalls involved with ranking. Both involve competition run amok: a ranking can encourage election administrators (1) to compete along the wrong dimensions, and (2) to cook the books. Each is thus some variant of a happiness problem. Competition is, of course, exactly what we do not have now, so both of these developments would be a heartening sign that the Index had gotten some traction. But competition can have perverse consequences if the Index is poorly designed.

Competing along the Wrong Dimensions

Rankings are designed to spur healthy competition, but they can sometimes cause people to compete along the wrong dimensions. When a poorly designed index starts to get traction, it can lead institutions to do unproductive, even silly things, to improve their standing.

Academics are especially quick to identify this problem because they have long lived with the *U.S. News & World Report* rankings,[23] which are infamous for causing foolishness of all sorts. Say the word "ranking" to a law professor, and she will immediately remind you of all the ridiculous ploys that schools have used to improve their standing. Columbia Law School, for instance, pushed its faculty to take their leaves in the spring rather than the fall because student-teacher ratios are assessed only in the fall. As a result, the school had to hire thirty-two part-time teachers to accommodate spring teaching needs.[24] In order to jack up its score on student expenditures, the University of Illinois's law school counted the fair market value of its students' Westlaw/Lexis subscriptions (which toted up to a cool $8.78 million). Given that both research services heavily discount their fees in order to woo future users, that "expenditure" was eighty times what Illinois actually paid.[25] Stanford Law School's entrepreneurial dean, Larry Kramer, has devoted part of his deanship to convincing the central university to let the law school "write a check" for its utilities rather than have the university deduct them automatically from student tuition. The reason for this accounting switch? It would allow the law school to count these expenses as student expenditures.[26] "The notion that I'm losing students because of this is insane," Kramer told the *New York Times*.[27]

If the Democracy Index were poorly designed, it could lead to as much silliness as the *U.S. News & World Report* rankings, creating problems that are more serious than the accounting hocus-pocus described above. Take fraud. Most voters care about fraud, so it would be perfectly sensible to include a fraud metric in the Index. The question, however, is how to measure fraud without creating perverse incentives. We don't want unsubstantiated fraud prosecutions or roving posses of state officials' accosting voters outside of polling places. These techniques have long been associated with vote suppression, and one would hardly want to give partisan officials an excuse to use them.

The Index might also create more systemic problems. Returning to Esty's mantra that "we measure what matters," we can't always measure everything that matters. Data-driven analysis creates a risk that people will neglect important issues that can't be captured in a statistic.[28] Some data will be too costly to gather; some issues will be too difficult to quantify. A ranking might lead states to compete on the things that can be measured while ignoring those that can't. Imagine, for instance, that it is too difficult to assess whether a registration system is easy for voters to navigate. States might be reluctant to put money into building a better registration system when they can improve their score, even if only marginally, by investing in something else.

Mitigating Strategies

There are, of course, strategies one can use to reduce the likelihood of foolish competition. The first is regular reevaluation and revision of the Index. If and when a problem arises, the designers of the Index should do their best to identify a metric that will redirect competitive energies into more productive channels.

A second strategy for avoiding foolish competition is to create a comprehensive Index. Because the extant data are sparse, early versions of the Index are likely to be narrow in scope and will not cover every aspect of the election process. A sparse Index has its virtues, but there are costs associated with parsimony. If there are only a handful of metrics in the Index, it is easier to improve one's standing by focusing on one or two. Further, if many aspects of election administration are left out of the Index, a state can easily divert resources from the parts of its system that aren't being measured to the parts that are.

Consider the examples noted above. If a state tried to increase its fraud score by engaging in techniques that deterred voters from casting a ballot, it might lower its score on any "ease of voting" metrics included in the Index. Comprehensiveness might similarly help with the problem of resource diversion. The more that is measured, the fewer tasks the state can neglect with impunity. For instance, returning to the example above, if the state neglects its registration system, it may find that lots of voters—mistakenly thinking that they've properly registered—will show up to vote. That would create administrative headaches for poll workers and longer lines for properly registered voters, problems that would reduce the state's overall score.

Do the Costs Outweigh the Benefits?

Here again, the costs and benefits associated with ranking are flip sides of the same coin. An index encourages election officials to compete along the dimensions it measures. If the ranking is well designed, this is all to the good. "Teaching to the test" is a problem, however, if the test is poorly designed.

In order to figure out whether teaching to the test is a problem, we need to know whether it's a good test and what kind of teaching takes place when there's no test. Right now, we are in a world with no test; we lack even the most basic data for evaluating the performance of our election system. If the Index works, it will surely reorient state and local priorities, perhaps causing them to neglect concerns that the Index doesn't measure. The cost might be significant enough to eschew data-driven analysis if the most of the basic components of election administration can't be captured in a statistic. We're back to the question, "As opposed to what?" A well-designed Democracy Index is surely better than the alternative . . . a world without data, one with no test at all.

Cheating

A final potential cost associated with ranking is cheating. The worry is that states will cook the books to improve their rankings. Like the concern about states' competing along the wrong dimensions, this worry is a variant of the happiness problem. If the Democracy Index were having such a powerful effect on election officials that they were tempted to cheat, we would already have come a long way. Nonetheless, for the Index to be a trustworthy guide for voters, reformers, and policymakers, the underlying data must be dependable.

Consider, for instance, a potential problem with the mini-Index I offered in chapter 2, which ranks states based on how much data they disclosed to the EAC. As I noted there, the Index accepts state disclosures at face value; it doesn't inquire whether the data provided are accurate. I made that choice out of necessity; it would require an army of political scientists to assess the underlying accuracy of each piece of data in the EAC survey. At present, that judgment represents a defensible compromise. Because states were unaware that they would be ranked when they responded to the EAC survey, there was little incentive to cheat at the time the survey was assembled. Should people begin to put pressure on the states about their disclosure rates, however, future rankings will have to create a system for verifying the validity of the underlying data.

Mitigating Strategies

There are two obvious strategies for dealing with the problem of cheating. The first is to rely on data from outside sources whenever possible. Voter surveys, for instance, can provide a pretty good mechanism for gathering basic data on many parts of the election process. "Testers" can similarly help us evaluate information that is otherwise in the state's control.

For the pieces of data that can come only from the state, the obvious solution to cheating is verification. For example, one strategy for double-checking state disclosures is random sampling. Random sampling might be prohibitively expensive on a large scale. But it can be used to spot-check state data from time to time. In spot-checking state disclosures, designers of the Index might even be able to piggyback on existing research. Political scientists spend a good deal of time using random samples to investigate basic questions about how the election system works, and the designers of the Index could use that research as an outside check on internal state reporting.

The designers of the Democracy Index could also follow the lead of other Index architects, who rely on many sources to verify information passed on by state officials. The designers of the Government Performance Project, for instance, use a triangulation strategy, asking the same question of many different actors in the state.[29] Similarly, the architects of the Democracy Index might talk to local polling officials, civil-rights watchdogs, and local reporters to identify problems that have gone unreported by state officials. This sort of qualitative read should help designers of the Index figure out whether they are working with decent quantitative information.

If Congress decides to mandate that states disclose performance data, something I discuss in chapter 5, it could also create backstops against cheating. Congress might, for instance, require states to certify the data or obtain an outside expert's blessings, just corporations are required to do under the Sarbanes-Oxley Act.[30]

Finally, designers of the Index could use the ranking system to punish states for faking the data. The people who put together the Environmental Performance Index, for instance, routinely toss data that don't seem plausible.[31] A state that is caught cooking the books could be punished by imputing the lowest possible number for the relevant portion of the ranking. Or the Democracy Index could include a "disclosure" component that would reward states that adopt the sort of certification practices described above.

The Right Approach to the Problem of Cheating

Cheating may be the most difficult problem posed by ranking. It is hard to detect and thus costly to avoid. While cheating would in some ways be a sign of the ranking's success—no one would bother to cheat if the Index didn't matter—it would also jeopardize the Index's power in the long run. The "As opposed to what?" question is tougher here, too. It is hard to argue that it's better to have states rampantly cheating to improve their rankings than not to have a ranking system at all.

There are a few reasons not to throw in the towel, however. Cheating is most likely to happen when the Index is getting traction—when it is starting to affect debates and influence behavior. And the more traction the Index gets, the more reasons that foundations and Congress will have to invest in it, perhaps providing the resources necessary to create alternative sources of data or better policing strategies. Further, the more comprehensive the Index becomes, the harder it will be to fake enough data to affect the state's ranking. If the only metrics on which the state performs well are those that involve self-reporting, people will suspect that something is afoot. To put it differently, as the Index grows in importance, its designers should have more tools available to police the cheating that might accompany that growth.

CONCLUSION

If we take a hard look at the costs associated with ranking, it is clear that they are genuine and genuinely important. The question is whether, in light of these costs, the game is still worth the candle.

We cannot answer that question by evaluating these trade-offs in the abstract. We have to think about how they play out in the real world, and that means answering another question, "As opposed to what?" In the abstract, the costs seem quite weighty: rankings are accorded more objectivity than they deserve, they can place pressure on the wrong people, they can encourage institutions to compete along the wrong dimensions, and they create an incentive for cheating. But the *real-world* alternative is one in which voters rest their decisions on far sillier shorthand, election officials feel almost no pressure to change, localities have few incentives to compete, and there isn't any test to cheat on. Editorial writer Meg Greenfield once observed, "Everybody's for democracy—in principle. It's only in practice that the thing gives rise to stiff objections."[32] It's just the reverse for rankings. It's easy to be against rankings in principle. It's only in practice that they start to look good.

5 Getting from Here to There in Miniature

Making the Democracy Index a Reality

Most of this book has been devoted to explaining why the Democracy Index should help us get from "here to there" in reforming our election system, changing the terrain on which reform battles are fought. Here I'll talk about getting from here to there in miniature—how to make the Democracy Index a reality. As with any other reform proposal, we cannot just add water and hope a Democracy Index will spring up. Even a modest reform like this one will take work to bring it to life. In this chapter, I'll discuss movement thus far, analyze the key challenges involved in assembling a Democracy Index, and lay out the steps we should take. The first half of the chapter is devoted to what are largely political questions (smoothing the way for data collection, creating an Index that will succeed in this political environment); the second half addresses the methodological challenges (creative strategies for getting the numbers we need, suggested metrics).

MOVEMENT THUS FAR

At the time of this writing, developments on the Democracy Index suggest grounds for genuine optimism. I first proposed creating a Democracy Index in the *Legal Times* in early 2007. Within two months, Senators Hillary Clinton and Barack Obama each put the idea into proposed legislation. Within the year, Congress set aside $10 million to fund the efforts of five states to improve their data-collection processes. During the same period, foundations and think tanks have organized several meetings to discuss the proposal. The idea has attracted keen interest from several foundations, including the Pew Trusts' Center on the States, which has played a leading role in improving state governance and promoting data-driven decision-making. Needless to say, reform proposals rarely get this kind of attention so quickly. The fact that so much has happened in such a short time suggests that the Democracy Index has a fighting chance.

It is not a coincidence that the Index has attracted the attention of two top-tier presidential candidates and major foundations. People are hungry for new ideas to get reform moving in this country. The Democracy Index offers a fresh vision of reform, one that shifts away from traditional civil-rights rhetoric toward a results-oriented, data-driven approach. Most reform proposals adopt a top-down, command-and-control approach to reform. The Democracy Index, in contrast, would allow us to improve the election system without Congress issuing a single regulation, leaving room for experimentation and innovation at the local level. Most reform appeals to the political interests of one party or another. The Democracy Index, in contrast, emphasizes transparency and accountability, values that ought to elicit support from both sides of the aisle. None of these differences guarantees the Index will come to pass. But they certainly suggest that the Index has a better chance of succeeding than most proposals for change.

NEXT STEPS
The Political Front

There are a variety of things we can do to improve the chances that the Index will succeed. Needless to say, the most important task that lies ahead is to pull together reliable comparative data on state and local performance, an issue I will discuss in the second half of this chapter. But proponents of the Index should also think hard about the best strategies for assembling and selling it.

Smoothing the Way for Data Collection

The most significant obstacle to creating an Index is the shocking dearth of data on how well our system is working. We will need more and better data to build a Democracy Index, and there are a number of strategies we can deploy to reach that goal.

Identifying the data we need. As is clear from the discussion in chapter 1, we need to do a good deal more work before we will have a precise sense of what data we need to build the Democracy Index. This will require proponents of the Index not only to consult with experts, election administrators, and policymakers, but to survey public opinion and consult with political and media experts

Happily, several important steps are being taken in that direction. The Pew Center on the States has run two conferences to identify what data a jurisdiction would collect if it were "serious about performance," to use Lynn Olson's phrase. The goal of these conferences is to lay down a marker about what kind of data jurisdictions ought to be collecting routinely.

Congress's model data-collection program should also be very useful in this regard. The lessons learned in those five states will tell us a good deal about what data can be collected and the most efficient strategies for doing so. It will also help us develop the software and infrastructure necessary to help other states establish data-collection programs of their own.

Raising awareness. At the same time that we are figuring out what data we need to assemble an Index, it is crucial to raise awareness about the need for better data.

Here again, Pew has started moving forward on this front. It is putting together a an assessment of state data-collecting practices that should be superior to the one I offered in chapter 2. My ranking "contracted out" the judgment calls about what data should be collected by relying on the EAC's judgment. Pew, in contrast, is getting input from the EAC, election administrators, reformers, and political scientists about what data matter and how to weight them. My index, out of necessity, focused only on state disclosures to the EAC. Pew will unleash a small army of trained staffers to examine whether the states make that information accessible to the public.

Modeling success. Another useful technique for building support is to create small-scale models of the Index to show how it works in the real world. Congress's effort to fund model data-collection programs among the states is a good example. It is very hard for critics to claim data collection can't be done when several states are already doing it.

It would be similarly useful to create a miniversion of the Democracy Index to get a sense of whether and how it will work. One option would be to create a Democracy Index for a single state, ranking localities against one another. Presumably an entrepreneurial secretary of state would value the opportunity to take part in the experiment. She'd be able to get much-needed resources to update the state's information systems. The Index would offer her a tool to put pressure on outlier localities to do better. And the secretary of state could certainly trumpet her participation in this innovative, data-driven experiment during her next run for office.

Alternatively, designers of the Index might create a small version of the Democracy Index by picking four or five important metrics and ranking all of the states on that basis. This strategy, too, would give designers of the Index a sense of whether and how the Index will affect the policymaking environment. Seeing how a small-scale version of the Index works might also help generate the support necessary to create a larger one.

Eliminating barriers to data collection. Another item on the "to do" list of the Index's supporters is to eliminate existing barriers to data collection. In a number of states regulations now prevent us from gathering the information we need to create an Index. Ohio, for instance, bans election observers in polling places,[1] something that would make it impossible to use randomly placed observers to record basic information about how well the state's election process is working.

Thad Hall has proposed that we address this problem by creating a "Transparency Index," which would rank the states based on how open the election process is. Like the Democracy Index, the Transparency Index might produce a useful shaming device to encourage states to do better.

Another important obstacle to data collection is the lack of standardization. Jurisdictions use markedly different terms and protocols in classifying data. The people who ran the EAC's Election Day Survey are excruciatingly familiar with this problem. Almost every section of the report mentions the issue. Without standard definitions, data collection is likely to be a meaningless exercise. Election administration is desperately in need of a lingua franca.

The EAC is particularly well suited to create those universal terms. Administering the Election Day Survey has given its staff more information than anyone else has about the source of the problem. As the federal agency charged with monitoring federal elections, it also enjoys the regulatory authority to devise standard definitions and disseminate them among states and localities.

Getting Election Administrators to Buy In

If we want to collect performance data from states and localities, it is crucial that we persuade election administrators that the game is worth the candle. If election administrators don't take data collection seriously, we won't get serious data from them.

Some of the resistance we see from election administrators may simply come from a lack of familiarity. Over the course of my interviews, I began to notice that many of the leaders on the data-collection front came from jobs where data collection is routine. Gary Smith moved to elections from the corporate world. Tammy Patrick drew on her background in sales. Bob Murphy was a computer junkie before he got involved in election administration. Joe Mansky started out as a scientist. For him—as for these other leaders in the field—looking at data was the most natural strategy for "making sense of the world."[2]

Familiarizing election officials with data collection is not going to be enough. The source of resistance runs deeper. No one likes to be evaluated, and resistance to monitoring seems to be particularly prevalent among election administrators. Consider what happened when the Election Assistance Commission was first created. Although the commission was underfunded and had no enforcement powers, the National Association of Secretaries of State demanded that Congress dismantle it even before all of its members had been appointed. The episode had the flavor of Hera sending snakes to kill Hercules in his cradle.

To overcome the resistance of election administrators, we must be able to make the case that data collection is in their interest. If we can't answer the question so many election administrators posed to me—"What are you going to do with all that data?"—we're unlikely to get the assistance we need from election folks. I've already talked about a few of the reasons why data matter to the lives of elections officials. Data can help election administrators do a better job, which is why it's so important to showcase the innovative programs I've talked about in this book. Data can also help election administrators put pressure on the state legislators and local commissioners for resources. The comparative data the Index would supply would also make strong election performance visible, rewarding election administrators for their successes.

Perhaps most importantly, as savvy election administrators have begun to realize, good data can serve as shield for election officials in today's heated political environment. Election administrators may not liked being evaluated, but the fact is that they are *already* being evaluated. The problem is that they are being judged in an information vacuum, something that all but guarantees that people will draw the wrong conclusions. As I noted in chapter 3, in a world without data, where voters become aware of problems only when there's a crisis, it's natural to connect the dots. Voters see a problem, the problem isn't visible elsewhere, and the election official usually has a partisan affiliation. It's all too easy to conclude the crisis has been caused by partisan shenanigans rather than deferred maintenance. As Matt Damschroder observes, any appointment system in which one "get[s] to have a position because of one's partisan affiliation" will create the impression that the "office is being run in a partisan manner."[3]

There's little an administrator can say in response to these accusations, as she has no means to establish her professional credentials or competence. We are quickly back to the "am not, are too" debate that no one can referee.

Things have deteriorated in the wake of the 2000 and 2004 controversies over the presidential elections. An outspoken subset of the reform community has begun to treat election administrators "as if they were co-conspirators to hand elections over to the Republican party,"[4] says one close observer. If election administrators were capable of even a fraction of the machinations attributed to them, they would make Machiavelli look like a rank amateur. Demonization is just too easy in a world without data.

While election administrators assume that the Democracy Index will serve as a sword for reformers, they often miss the fact that it will simultaneously provide them a shield. A ranking system that showed that a locality ran one of the best election systems in the country would go far to defend against unfair accusations. Even a ranking system that showed that a jurisdiction was near the bottom of the list might be useful, as voters would see that other jurisdictions suffered from the same problems. It would be easier to understand that the problem is caused by deferred maintenance, not partisan malice.

Think about some of the people I've talked about in this book. For example, L.A. County's Conny McCormack and Franklin County's Matt Damschroder have both been excoriated at some point by reform groups (McCormack for her defense of punch-card ballots and, later, touch-screen voting systems;[5] Damschroder for the debacle that took place in Franklin County in 2004).[6] Both also enjoy a great deal of respect from experts and other election administrators. Tom Mann, a senior fellow at the Brookings Institute, recently praised L.A. County as one of the best-run systems in the country because of McCormack's "extraordinarily competent leadership."[7] And Damschroder was elected president of the Ohio Association of Election Officials[8] and is held in high regard by people knowledgeable about Ohio's system. Regardless whether you think McCormack and Damschroder are villains or heroes, it is hard to know if you are correct in a world without data. The Democracy Index would at least help the conversation start at the right place.

Savvy election administrators have begun to catch on to the fact that data can serve as a shield when a controversy occurs. Tammy Patrick told me about the role that Maricopa County's election tracking system played during Arizona's 2008 presidential primary election.[9] Contrary to usual practice, the primaries were closed, which meant that only registered Democrats could vote in the Democratic primary and only registered Republicans could vote in the Republican primary. Unsurprisingly, a number of independent voters were (properly) turned away. Because people didn't understand why they were being turned away, rumors began to fly. For instance, one radio show claimed that thousands of Hispanic voters had been improperly purged from the registration lists. Maricopa's tracking system enabled the county to figure out exactly what was going on and quickly share the information with the press. "It made a huge difference," says Patrick.

We saw a similar story in L.A. County during the presidential primaries. Because of a badly designed ballot, voters who weren't registered as members of a party in Los Angeles had to fill in two bubbles if they wanted to vote for a presidential candidate in the Democratic primary. Reports indicated that thousands, perhaps hundreds of thousands of voters had failed to fill in both bubbles. Accusations began to fly that the "double bubble" problem would end up costing Barack Obama delegates in the hotly contested race. As is always the case with election controversies, people were quick to raise questions about political mischief. L.A. County responded by doing statistical sampling and putting the data online to show that most voters filled out the ballots properly and that the number of voters who had failed to do so, while large, was not enough to affect the outcome of the race.[10] In the words of Kim Alexander, president of the California Voter Foundation, L.A. County's efforts "quelled the controversy."[11]

As these examples suggest, transparency is a powerful weapon in politics, and good data are the "antidote to anecdote," in the words of Steve Weir, the county clerk-recorder for Contra Costa County.[12] That's just why one major election official with whom I spoke is considering hiring a full-time numbers cruncher on the staff to help his office sort through controversies like these.

When I talk about these stories with election officials, they often nod their heads in agreement but continue to worry about the misuse of data. Even if election officials have good data, they worry that their critics will be able to twist those numbers. After all, few jurisdictions can afford a full-time number cruncher on their stuff to respond to unfounded accusations.

Political scientists could help allay these worries by agreeing to referee controversies over the data, serving as the teched-up equivalent of factcheck.org. At present, political scientists ask a lot of favors of election administrators, who provide the information scholars need for their research (academics are always grateful to the person who helped them get tenure). So how about a quid pro quo? If election administrators start providing better, publicly available data, political scientists should agree to help sort out data controversies that swirl around elections. This already happens informally. In the wake of the 2004 election, for instance, study after study emerged purporting to show that the election was stolen. Political scientists would vet each paper, figure out what was wrong with it, and calm the waters by telling reporters and talking heads not to trust it.

Finally, even if bureaucratic resistance to data collection is close to an immovable object, data-driven policymaking is likely to be an irresistible force. Programs like CitiStat have begun to sweep through local and state governments, and election administration lends itself to measurement in ways that many state-run services do not. Whether or not the Democracy Index is assembled, we will see a push for data. Jonah Goldman of the National Campaign for Fair Elections notes that reformers have been trying to "cobble together" good data "with duct tape" for a long time.[13] The same is true of reformers with a conservative bent, as is evident from the fight over voter ID.

Ray Martinez, the former EAC commissioner, is not worried about the problem of bureaucratic resistance. He has seen a new generation of election administrators taking over. They are "younger, more technologically savvy, less resistant to change, and looking for help"—just the kind of people who ought to find the Democracy Index attractive. "The reasons why reform is hard are going away," says Martinez. "They are retiring."[14]

Getting the Data

Once we identify the data we want, raise awareness about its importance, and smooth the path for data collection, there are two obvious routes for obtaining the data. The first would look to Congress to mandate and fund good data collection. The second would rely on a private foundation to gather the information we need.

FEDERAL MANDATES

The most straightforward strategy for creating an Index would be for Congress to pass something like Senator Obama's or Senator Clinton's proposed bill. If the federal government required states to disclose most of the data necessary to create the Index, it would be fairly easy for a well-respected, nonpartisan organization like the Pew Center on the States or the AEI/Brookings Election Reform Project to assemble it into an Index.

Money, money, money. Needless to say, Congress needs to do more than wave its regulatory wand for good data to appear. First, Congress should give localities the money they need to collect the information. As Thad Hall and Dan Tokaji have pointed out, federal elections "are the country's oldest unfunded mandate."[15] States and localities run federal elections without receiving adequate resources to do so. Congress should not impose yet another duty on these jurisdictions without providing more resources. It should heed Hall and Tokaji's advice by trading states "money for data." As Secretary of State Brunner notes, one of the main reasons that administrators resist change is that they are tired of fighting for the money they need to implement it. She argues that the most effective strategy for getting good data is to make money available to collect it.[16]

A key question, of course, is how much the Democracy Index will cost. We don't yet have enough information to put a price tag on the Index, and anything I offered here would the worst sort of seat-of-the-pants calculation. One of the most important things that will come from Congress's innovative effort to fund model data-collection efforts at the state level is a number. Putting a price tag on data collection is essential if you want Congress to fund it.

We may, of course, discover that data collection is so costly that the game is not worth the candle. But I doubt it. While the start-up costs will be significant, it's important to keep in mind that there are economies of scale here. Maricopa County's sophisticated, real-time monitoring system cost about $14,000 to create, but only a fraction of that to maintain. If, as I suggest in the next section, a foundation or Congress were to "think like a computer programmer" and create a master software program that jurisdictions could download and adapt for free, a good chunk of the start-up costs for data collection would be eliminated. And once data collection becomes a routine practice, the costs of collecting data will decline.

Routine data collection, of course, still costs real money. Will that price tag be prohibitively high? Perhaps. But keep in mind that corporations, where the bottom line is all that matters, think the benefits outweigh the costs. So, too, do the countless government agencies that collect data to inform their policymaking. Perhaps some of this is information for information's sake. But the data-collection trendline suggests otherwise.

It's not enough for Congress to trade money for data. It should also supplement its monetary carrots with regulatory sticks. It ought to learn from the mistakes it made with HAVA, where it failed to provide adequate enforcement mechanisms. At a minimum, Congress should grant the EAC regulatory authority to punish localities for failing to collect the numbers we need.

A skeptic might think there is little chance that the Index will garner congressional support. While it would be foolish to predict that anything will be enacted by Congress, the Index's long-term chances are fairly good. As noted, Senators Barack Obama and Hillary Clinton have already put the idea into proposed legislation. Both presidential candidates, Obama and John McCain, have long been interested in election reform (Obama even taught election law at the University of Chicago). Moreover, reform is a notoriously crisis-driven industry. When the next crisis comes—as it inevitably will—politicians will be looking for something to do. The Democracy Index has a better chance than most proposals of getting adopted when members of Congress are ready to appear reform-minded. After all, it seems more likely that Congress will ask states to disclose basic information about how the election system is run than to regulate state election systems top-down, as most reformers propose.

Moreover, precisely because the Democracy Index is an intermediate strategy—designed to change the debates on reform rather than enact a particular kind of reform—it doesn't have an obvious political valence. It is not hard to figure out which party will be helped by a particular campaign finance law or a voter registration rule. A here-to-there proposal like the Democracy Index, in contrast, seems less likely to favor one party or another precisely because it is one step removed from substantive proposals. It's just the kind of proposal capable of garnering widespread support.

Private support. Even if the skeptic is correct that Congress will not pass legislation to mandate data collection, a private foundation could fund the creation of a good portion of the data that we would want for the Index. As I note in the next section, a foundation could commission surveys, hire observers and testers, create a network of "Nielsen voters," or hire experts to evaluate how each system is working. A foundation could also persuade researchers to tweak existing studies to get the data we need.[17]

As to the remaining information we'd need to assemble an Index—the data that a private foundation could not independently produce—a private foundation should have the political muscle and moral standing to call jurisdictions to account for not disclosing basic performance data. By laying down a marker for what data jurisdictions should collect, a private foundation could push election administrators in the right direction. Remember the Quality Counts educational report. It began in a world without data, but it has gradually shamed school systems into collecting better information. So, too, the Environmental Performance Index has helped push nation-states to do a better job collecting information on environmental performance. The development of these indexes suggests a modified version of the *Field of Dreams* mantra: if you build it, they will come around.[18]

The Election Assistance Commission is likely to be a useful ally in this regard. It is a commission in search of a mission, and data collection is the most obvious mission to choose. As election insiders are well aware, the EAC has been politically embattled since its inception. Although Congress intended the commission to improve how elections are run, it gave the new agency a modest mandate, little money, and less clout. As I noted in chapter 2, two years after the EAC was created, Congress hadn't yet given it an operating budget, which means that it didn't have an office and had to hold its first meetings at a Starbucks.[19] If you want to get a sense of how precarious a position the EAC has occupied, talk to Ray Martinez, one of its first commissioners. He'll tell you about moving a young family to Washington, D.C., and worrying every night that the agency wouldn't have enough money to pay his salary.[20]

As Martinez acknowledges, the "biggest challenge" for the EAC has been to make itself "relevant."[21] And the one thing that this embattled agency has been able to do since its creation is gather data. The EAC's Election Day Survey has already moved us closer to being able to assemble an Index, and that survey should become even more useful as states get into the habit of responding to it. Moreover, the EAC has every incentive to do better on the data-collection front. Agencies always have to explain their existence to Congress to get the funding they need. Information gathering is a pretty good justification for the EAC's existence. Who, after all, is against sunshine? Data collection is a mission that places the EAC beyond political reproach while serving a genuinely useful purpose.

Selling the Index

The final political task for designers of the Index will be to sell it. There are, of course, obvious public relations challenges associated with introducing the Index—creating a website, generating press, educating the public, disseminating it to policymakers.

Here I want to talk about a less obvious, but no less important, strategy for selling the Index: politicking. Perhaps the most important thing that designers of the Index can do to sell the Index after it's assembled is to spend a lot of time talking about the choices that go into the Index *before* it's assembled. As corny as it sounds, talking things through is crucially important in this context. The Index will incorporate a number of value judgments, and its success will depend on widespread acceptance. It is therefore essential that the Index's architects hear what other people—voters, election administrators, academics, policymakers—think about the choices being made.

Academics unthinkingly translate admonitions to "talk things through" as an instruction to "deliberate"[22]—to engage in respectful debate, offering arguments that any reasonable person can accept. That's not what I mean. Though reasoned deliberation is all to the good, the Index's architects should also engage in what partisans call politicking and corporate executives call market research. For instance, the Index's architects should use polling and focus groups to be sure that they are including metrics that appeal to most voters. They should try to get a sense from seasoned politicians whether placing this or that metric in the Index will trip it up politically, perhaps asking Republican or Democratic operatives how they would sink the Index in a debate. Given that election administrators are likely to play a crucial role in implementing the Index, its architects should be sure that they are focusing on measures that administrators can live with.

It might seem distasteful to engage in even a modest amount of politicking when designing the Index. A purist might insist that the Index should be based entirely on the views of experts, who are distant from the political fray and immune to the exigencies of day-to-day politics. It would be a mistake, however, to quarantine the Index from the concerns of everyday politics.[23] For the Index to work in the real world, it is going to have to survive in a political swamp. It is therefore crucial that we inoculate it against the diseases that infest that unfortunate terrain. A little bit of politicking can go a long way in helping change take root.

Politicking is also important for a more idealistic reason. Designers of the Index are going to make a number of normative choices about how elections systems should be run. Rather than handing down those decisions from on high, they ought to pay attention to the stakeholders in this debate—voters, reformers, politicians, and election administrators.

None of this is to say that the integrity of the Index should be so compromised that it is rejected by experts in the field. The Index needs the support of experts in order to succeed. But it should be possible to inoculate it against political opposition without risking a full-blown political infection. Here, again, the key is to strike the right balance.

ASSEMBLING THE INDEX

If we want to get the Democracy Index from "here to there," we'll have to address not just political obstacles, but methodological ones. How exactly, will we collect the numbers we need to build the Index, and what kinds of metrics should we choose?

In chapter 1, I offered a preliminary sketch of what a Democracy Index ought to look like. In this section, I'll talk more about the challenges involved in creating an Index and the methodologies and metrics that its architects Index might use. Anyone hoping to find a full blueprint Index in this chapter will be disappointed, however. As I explained in chapter 1, it would be foolhardy to try to describe the Index in intimate detail at this early stage. We don't yet know how crucial stakeholders—voters, election administrators, policymakers—think about these questions. We don't yet know what kind of data will be available when the Index is first assembled. We don't yet know what Congress's model program will tell us about the costs involved in collecting the data. Assembling an Index will involves a pushmi-pullyu process, requiring us to toggle between the real and the ideal. Until we know more about the "real" side of the equation, a finely detailed blueprint would serve little purpose. It would bear an uncomfortable resemblance to the old joke about how many economists it takes to change a lightbulb. The answer is two: one to change the lightbulb, and one to assume the existence of a ladder.[24]

Rather than assume the existence of a ladder and pretend that a yet-to-be-identified set of data will exist at the yet-to-be-specified time the Index is created, here I'll work through some of the broader implementation questions involved in designing an Index. While I won't provide a detailed blueprint, I will describe the basic building materials available to the Index's architects.

The Ideal

As I noted in chapter 1, the Index should measure three simple things—registration, balloting, counting—using hard data and performance measures. Ideally, we'd like numbers to evaluate whether (1) every eligible voter who wants to register can do so, (2) every registered voter who wants to cast a ballot can do so, and (3) every ballot cast is counted properly.[25]

Now that you've had a crash course in election administration, you might notice that the performance goals I describe bear some resemblance to the residual vote rate, the elegant metric that political scientists in the Caltech/MIT Voting Project created to assess whether too many ballots were getting discarded. It's not a perfect metric, but it offers a good proxy for figuring out whether there is a problem with voting machines. The three basic performance categories I suggest might be thought of as a residual registration rate, a residual balloting rate, and a residual counting rate.*

If we could assess residual rates for registration, balloting, and counting, we would have a close-to-ideal set of metrics. These metrics wouldn't, of course, capture everything we want to assess. For instance, we'd want to be sure that the voters being registered are eligible, and we'd want to be sure that the ballots being counted were cast by eligible voters. Nonetheless, if we could measure these three performance goals, we would be well on our way toward assembling an Index. The metrics are easy to explain and justify. They offer us hard numbers, not qualitative assessments. They measure performance outputs (how well is the system actually working?) rather than policy inputs (what policies do we think work best?). They give us a basic read on each part of the process—both how easy voters find voting to be, and whether the state is doing its part. Finally, they heed MIT political scientist Charles Stewart's wise suggestion that it is better to measure a few things well than to measure many things badly.[26]

Getting to the Ideal

Needless to say, we ain't there yet. Some states don't even track the residual vote rate. Getting even a rough sense of roll-off—the number of people who try to register or vote but fail—during each part of the process is obviously much harder. For this reason, in assembling the Democracy Index 1.0, we'll have to find real-world proxies for capturing the information we'd want in an ideal world. Here again, though, the biggest obstacle is getting the data.

*Someone might sensibly object that the "best" registration or balloting system will not be able to register *every* eligible voter or help *every* voter cast a ballot. Remember the dark secret of election administration—no election system is perfect. It may not be cost-effective or even possible to create a system that prevents every type of voter error. Even if we think an excellent system would have some roll-off, however, ranking builds that into the equation. A Democracy Index doesn't hold jurisdictions up to an ideal standard but measures them against one another. There's no need to debate what the optimal roll-off is because that number will, in effect, be folded into the comparison for every state.

As I noted above, there are two avenues for collecting the numbers we need: (1) mandated or voluntarily disclosure by states and localities, and (2) private efforts. Here, I'll talk about the here-to-there question for both strategies. I'll explain how we can make it easier for states and localities to collect the information we need, and I'll show that there are a variety of means to gather information that don't depend on state or local disclosures.

Making It Easier for State and Localities to Disclose Information

Needless to say, no matter how varied our strategy for collecting data, if we are going to evaluate election systems based on performance, there is some information that we'd like state and localities to disclose. So how can we make it easier for states and localities to collect the numbers we want?

Think like the Census Bureau. If you want to think creatively about reducing the costs of data collection, you should talk to Eric Fischer, the Congressional Research Service analyst who speaks as knowledgeably about hermaphroditic sharks as John Bolton's adolescence. In thinking about the challenges involved in gathering data, Fischer argues that it's a mistake to think that we need massive amounts of data from every single jurisdiction to get a good read on whether the system is working. He suggests that anyone interested in collecting better election data should think like the Census Bureau.[27] The Census Bureau knows that it needs some kinds of information from everyone. It thus sends every household a "short form" once every ten years to ask basic demographic questions—age, sex, race, and ethnicity. The Bureau then sends a long form to a subset of the population to pull together more detailed data on issues like jobs, education, and housing.

The Democracy Index might similarly use a short form/long form approach. We could ask every jurisdiction to collect basic information. We could then use random sampling to glean the rest of the data we'd like to have. This strategy would reduce the burdens on election administrators, particularly those at the local level, while still giving us a good sense of how well the system is working.

Think like Congress. Another strategy for reducing the cost of data collection is to think like Congress. Many federal statutes—from Title VII to the Fair Labor Standards Act—exempt small businesses from their ambit.

There are some requirements that are just too onerous to place upon mom-and-pop businesses, instances where the game is indeed not worth the candle. The same may be true of election administration. There may be some cases where it makes sense to exempt the smallest localities from the reporting requirements we try to achieve elsewhere.

Think like Wal-Mart. Another simple strategy for collecting performance data is to follow the example of Wal-Mart. When you pay with a credit card at Wal-Mart, two messages pop up when you sign the signature key pad. The first is whether you are ready to accept the signature. The second is a simple question, like "Was the store clean today?" The survey is not intrusive; you can complete your purchase without answering the question. But it's easy to do, which means that it generates a lot of information about the conditions of Wal-Mart's stores.

Imagine applying the Wal-Mart solution in the elections context. A voter-registration form, for instance, might give voters the option of indicating how long it took them to procure and fill out the form. A voter receiving an optical scan ballot might be given one more sheet of paper with an optional question—How long did you spend in line? Was it easy to find your polling place today? Do you have any complaints about the service your poll worker provided? A computerized voting system might do the same, prompting voters after they'd approved their ballot to answer one more question. Although the numbers generated would not represent a purely random survey—we wouldn't expect everyone to answer the question at the same rates—it will target a much bigger population than most random surveys and thus provide sufficient quantities of data that political scientists could generate meaningful cross-jurisdictional comparisons.

Care to guess which election administrator already thinks like Wal-Mart? Gary Smith, of course, the businessman who "retired" by becoming the head of elections in Forsyth County, Georgia. When I told him about my Wal-Mart idea, he proudly showed me the survey card he distributes to voters. Smith says that the survey costs very little to administer and gets him lots of information on how well elections are running in his jurisdiction.[28]

Think like somebody who is ahead of the curve. The reason that collecting data on election performance is such a daunting task is that we don't do it now. Election administration is way behind the many other government agencies that collect information. That's the bad news. The good news is that there are some advantages to being behind the curve. Indeed, sometimes it's possible to be so far behind the curve that you are ahead of it.

One advantage to playing catch-up is that it's possible to learn from others' mistakes. We know a lot more about collecting data than we did twenty years ago. Think about Tammy Patrick's experience in Maricopa County. The county moved from relying on slips of paper to a state-of-the-art tracking system that resembled the databases Patrick saw while working in sales. Patrick was able to avoid beginners' mistakes, like failing to prepopulate the data and requiring too many keystrokes to enter the data. As Maricopa County's experiences show, the costs of transitioning to a robust data-collection process are real, but less significant than they would have been in prior years.

A second advantage to being behind the curve is that technology has improved dramatically, which means that it will be easier to put in place a workable system than it was even ten years ago. Call it the lesson of the African phone system. Many people used to worry that it would be impossible for developing countries in Africa to create a modern phone system. How would these poor countries obtain the resources and technology they needed to lay down phone lines to every home and business? Then came the cell phone, which doesn't require costly land lines or a complicated infrastructure. The result? Africa was able to make a remarkable advance in telecommunications without making the costly investments that more developed nations had made to get to roughly the same place.

We're also close to starting from scratch in collecting data on election performance. That means that we can put in a system that incorporates all the advantages that technology now affords rather than try to tweak the existing system to catch up with changing technology.

Think like a computer programmer. Few jurisdictions, of course, can afford to create a data-collection system from scratch, the way that Maricopa County did. But here's where we should think like a computer programmer and imagine developing the elections equivalent of GNU/Linux. Unlike Microsoft's operating system, GNU/Linux is free. Better yet, anyone can make changes to it, and then share those changes with others.

One of the advantages associated with being behind the curve is that the time is ripe for a foundation to create the rough cognate to GNU/Linux—a universal data-collection program that could be downloaded and modified for free by any jurisdiction. Creating a free, reliable software system to help jurisdictions collect data and share information would be a timely intervention in the process. And it's a good deal cheaper than asking each jurisdiction to build its own system separately.

Think like a mass transit official. Bob Murphy, the computer junkie turned election administrator, came up with another idea for making data-collection easier. "What you need," he told me, is "something like a Mass Transit Authority for collecting data."[29] It's easy to see the logic. As with transportation, data collection is an area where there are economies of scale. It's easier for a centralized authority to push for a mass transit system than to depend on every small town to act on its own. So, too, it's easier to build an information superhighway in the elections context if a centralized authority could coordinate efforts. As Murphy points out, mass transit authorities give cities and towns the leverage they need to get the job done. And they can save every small jurisdiction from having to reinvent the data-collection wheel by providing a model for everyone. Needless to say, the obvious candidate for serving this role will often be the secretary of state's office.

Private Sources of Performance Data

As I noted above, it is also possible to gather useful information on election performance without relying on states and localities to disclose it. Here are some examples of the strategies a private foundation could use to get the numbers we need for the Index.

Testers/observers. One promising solution for gathering performance data is to rely on testers. In *The Mystery of Capital*, Hernando DeSoto describes his elegant strategy for evaluating the quality of corporate regulations. He simply sent testers to different counties to try to register a business there. Based on their feedback, he gathered useful quantitative and qualitative data on how each process worked.[30]

Imagine we wanted to evaluate how well the registration system is working for citizens. Following DeSoto's example, we could send out a diverse group of eligible voters—someone who lives in a rural area, someone who lives in the inner city, someone who is blind, someone who has a seventh-grade education, someone who requires language assistance, an overseas voter—and see whether they are able to register and how long it takes them to do so.

Election observers could serve a similarly useful role. For instance, if you want to get a read on how well the balloting process is working, you could randomly assign observers to polling places and ask them to count how many people showed up at the wrong polling place or how many people tried to vote only to be told they weren't registered. Randomly placed observers could similarly record how long the lines were, whether the parking lot was full, and whether poll workers answered questions correctly.

Nielsen voters. Alternatively, imagine we created the voting equivalent of "Nielsen families,"[31] the individuals who record their television watching habits for the Nielsen ratings service. Designers of the Index could ask randomly selected voters to record information about their experiences with the election process. For instance, a Nielsen voter might be asked how long it took her to register, whether she thought her polling place was conveniently located, and whether she found the ballot design confusing. Alternatively, as MIT's Charles Stewart has suggested, designers of the Index might randomly tag some registration cards or ballots and follow them through the process.[32]

Voter surveys. Voter surveys also provide a useful strategy for gathering information on state performance. Asking a randomly sampled group of voters about their experience can generate a good deal of information about how the system is working. Voters could be asked whether they tried to register but failed, how hard it was to find their polling place, whether they encountered any problems with poll workers, and how long they stood in line.[33] Relying on voters' recollections may not give us a precise answer to these questions. For instance, voters may systematically under- or over-report certain problems. But all that matters for the Index is reliable comparative data. As long as voter recollections are not systematically skewed (that is, as long as voters in Idaho overreport by roughly the same amount as do voters in New York), the *comparative* information is still useful.

Imagine, for example, you want to get a sense of how well the registration system is working. In order to measure that in performance terms, you could use survey data to identify how many voters get lost in the registration process or learn that they are not properly registered when they show up at the polls.

Survey data won't give you a perfect read on how well the system is working. It might sweep in voters who think they are eligible to vote but aren't (and thus *should* be prevented registering by a well-functioning system). Further, we know that people sometimes misreport voting behavior (more people claim that they voted than actually vote), and postelection events (media reports, having one's preferred candidate lose) can affect what voters say when an election is over. But some of these problems can be fixed. You could conduct surveys right after the close of registration in order to reduce the effect of media coverage or election outcomes on self-reporting. Other problems drop out because we are comparing states to one another. For instance, if misreporting occurs at the same level across states, the problem falls away when we assess the data comparatively. While there are details yet to be worked out, a preliminary study by MIT's Charles Stewart offers some cautious optimism about the use of survey data for these purposes.[34]

Other Potential Metrics

Haven given you a general sense of the measurement strategies the architects of the Index might use to get the numbers they need, let me show you a representative sample of what experts think is achievable in the short term. All of these examples are drawn from discussions that took place during a 2007 conference on the Democracy Index sponsored by the Pew Center on the States, the Joyce Foundation, the AEI-Brookings Election Reform Project, and the Ohio State University Moritz College of Law. Over the course of the conference, political scientists, law professors, and election administrators brainstormed about what a Democracy Index should look like. At the end of the conference, the discussion had moved forward enough for the moderators to ask the experts each to name three reasonable metrics that are either available today or could be reasonably collected in the near future. The full list was enormous. Here's a sampling of the ones I thought were the most promising:

	Registration	*Balloting*	*Counting*
Performance goal	Every eligible voter who wants to register can do so	Every registered voter who wants to cast a ballot can do so.	Every ballot cast is counted properly.
Relevant values	Convenience, integrity, accuracy	Convenience and accuracy	Integrity and accuracy
Potential proxies	Survey data on how many voters encountered a problem registering Time it took to register (and success rate) based on testers or "Nielsen voters" or randomly tagged registration cards Number of voters who appeared to cast a ballot on Election Day but were told they were not registered Number of provisional ballots counted because registration was verified	Survey data on the length of lines, problems encountered in casting a ballot, poll worker complaints, how easy voters found it to find their polling place, how long it took to vote Time it took to cast a ballot (and success rate) based on "Nielsen voters" or randomly tagged ballots. Length of lines, number of voters turned away, and poll worker problems based on outside observers	Residual vote rate Number of ballots cast by ineligible voters Difference between election night count and canvas or difference between results of the recount/audit and state-certified vote Average number of days between Election Day and state-certified results

	Registration	*Balloting*	*Counting*
Potential proxies *(continued)*	Error rates assessed by comparing registration list to the death rolls or commercial mailing lists Percentage of errors in state registration database based on independent audits Time between submission of randomly chosen registration forms and entry into the state database Registration rates (if they can be adjusted to take into account factors outside an election administrator's control—such as socioeconomic conditions) Incremental changes in registration rates[1]	Use of time-stamped cards to determine how long voters stood in line Number and duration of voting machine breakdowns Average number of minutes polling places opened late Number of complaints reported on statewide hotlines Number of voters who left without casting a vote or provisional ballot Turnout rates (if they can be adjusted to take into account factors outside an election administrator's control—such as socioeconomic conditions) Incremental changes in turnout rates[2]	

[1]Registration and turnout rates vary for reasons that are outside an election administrator's control. Poor people register and turn out at a lower rate than wealthy people, and registration and turnout rates tend to go up when elections are competitive. If it's not possible to use regression analysis to "pull out" the effects of socioeconomic categories on these rates,

one might look to incremental changes in registration and turnout rates as an appropriate metric. For instance, imagine you picked a baseline—registration numbers from the last presidential election—and ranked states based on whether they were able to improve registration numbers by the next presidential race. The hope would be that such a measure would filter out socioeconomic factors and the effects of competition. The key, as with all metrics in the index, is to ensure that it does not pull in too many factors beyond an election administrator's control, becoming a measure of luck, not skill.

[2]See prior note to this table.

CONCLUSION

Though some of the steps involved in getting a Democracy Index from here to there may seem a bit daunting, it is worth asking once again, "As opposed to what?" The Democracy Index has garnered more support and made more progress than most proposals ever do. The ideas also seems easier to push through the process than most types of reform.

As to the biggest obstacle to creating the Index—collecting the data—it's worth taking the long view here. Election administrators are not the first people to face these problems. Every government agency that I discussed in chapter 2 began where we are now, in a world without data. The specific obstacles involved may differ, but this is not the first field to confront decentralization, limited resources, and measurement challenges.

Moreover, while the challenges involved in assembling an Index can be daunting, they are the same challenges faced by the designers of other successful indexes. Dan Esty still complains about the need for more environmental performance data. When the developers of the Quality Counts educational report began, few school systems collected even a fraction of the data necessary for a good performance Index. Today, most of them do. Over the course of the last two years, I have interviewed many people who have been involved in creating an Index. Every one of them started out worrying that the data-collection problems were insurmountable. And every one of them managed to move their projects from here to there.

Conclusion

Getting from "Here to There" Redux

Much of this book has been devoted to describing a promising new strategy for improving the way we run elections: a Democracy Index. The Democracy Index is a quintessentially here-to-there solution. It doesn't impose standards on how our elections are run. It doesn't take power away from partisan officials. It doesn't professionalize the bureaucracy that runs our elections. Instead, it pushes in the direction of better performance, less partisanship, and greater professionalism. By giving voters, policymakers, and election administrators the right information in the right form, it creates the conditions in which bigger and better reform is possible.

The New Style of Reform

The Index is of a piece with a larger shift in reform movement. *New York Times* editorialist David Brooks could be describing many of the people in this book when he writes about the new generation of social entrepreneurs:

> These thoroughly modern do-gooders dress like venture capitalists. They talk like them. They even think like them. . . . Almost willfully blind to ideological issues, they will tell you, even before you have a chance to ask, that they are data-driven and accountability-oriented.[1]

Ian Ayres has argued that "supercrunchers"—the masters of data-driven analysis—are involved in almost every aspect of our lives, from wine ratings to plane tickets. His book has made the *New York Times* best-seller list and is being translated into eleven languages. Cass Sunstein and Richard

Thaler have argued that the future path of reform is not top-down government mandates, but softer "nudges" that a government can provide by doing a better job of framing questions, choosing defaults, and providing decision-making shortcuts.

The Democracy Index mines a similar vein. Rather than relying upon a civil-rights enforcement strategy or a New Deal command-and-control approach, the Index deploys a data-driven, market-oriented approach. It is tailor-made for the new generation of election reformers like Spencer Overton, who fought the good fight on voter ID, or Dan Tokaji, the baseball nut who insists on hard numbers and "moneyball" reforms. The election reformers of this new generation may be unyielding in their idealism, but they are pragmatic in their approach. They are willing to look to a variety of institutions (the market, administrative agencies), not just the courts, for solutions. And they are as likely to appeal to hardheaded ideas—accountability, competition—as soft-hearted values like participation and empowerment.

Like Thaler and Sunstein's "nudge" approach, the Index provides better decision-making tools than we have now. It improves the policymaking process by creating better information shortcuts for voters, policymakers, and election administrators. The Index gives voters a better cue to cast a vote. It gives policymakers the shorthand they need to figure out whether a problem exists and how to fix it. It might even provide a professional touchstone for election administrators, helping identify the kinds of best practices that professionals have long used as a decision-making shortcut.

While the Index ought to shame policymakers and election officials into doing better, it is shaming of an unusual sort. It looks nothing like the collective "tut-tuts" that often slip from the mouths of academics, nor does it resemble the "Do more, do better" mantra that reformers must invoke in a world without data. Instead, the Index is a shaming device of a quite pragmatic sort. It does not turn on some ideal standard, but holds poor performers up to a realistic baseline, challenging them to do as well as their neighbors. It rests on the simple idea that showing something can be done is better than claiming it can be.

The Democracy Index reflects an equally pragmatic approach toward politics. Partisanship and localism provide powerful incentives that push against reform. Most reform efforts involve an effort to swim upstream against those powerful currents. The Democracy Index, in contrast, realigns partisan and local incentives by linking officials' political fates to their professional performance and giving top policymakers a reason to care about reform. Further, because the Index can serve as both sword and shield in partisan warfare, the Index should encourage the political parties to do the work of reform for us. It thus promises to change these vicious political cycles into virtuous ones.

Finally, in a world where reformers tend to look for national solutions to national problems, the Index turns decentralization to our advantage. One of the reasons change is hard to come by is that the election system is run by so many institutions (administrative agencies, legislatures, local boards) at so many levels of government (local, state, federal). A system like ours does have two advantages, however. First, it facilitates experimentation that will help us identify best practices and promising policies. Second, it allows us to appeal to an actor in one part of the system to help regulate actors in another part, thus mitigating the self-interest that usually short-circuits meaningful reform.

The Democracy Index takes advantage of both features of localism. It allows local jurisdictions to serve as laboratories of democracy while helping us disseminate the results of the most successful experiments. And it helps voters, policymakers, and election administrators do a better job of monitoring the system. The Democracy Index, in short, takes advantage of the most useful features associated with decentralization while avoiding its worst excesses.

A World with a Democracy Index

I've spent a lot of time in this book talking about what the reform environment looks like in a world without data. It's a world where everyone argues over which direction to go even though no one can map where we are now. Where calls for change are too often based on anecdotes and idealism. Where the reformer's mantra is "Do better, do more." Where voters have no means of refereeing the debates they hear. Where election officials can't assess their own performance, let alone figure out how to improve. Where politicians have every reason to ignore pleas for change. Where any election administrator hit by a turnout tsunami is at risk of being demonized. Where strong performance is ignored and failures are rarely noticed. Where election administrators have no means of finding the innovative needle in the policymaking haystack.

A world with a Democracy Index ought to look different. It would give us a map of where we are so we could chart where we want to go. Starry-eyed reformers would be able to speak in the cadence of corporate executives. Election administrators would have a lingua franca to describe the standards a well-functioning election system should meet. And voters and policymakers wouldn't need anyone to translate those debates for them because the Index would do it for them. A world with a Democracy Index should be one where politicians and election administrators are rewarded for doing well and feel pressured when they could do better. But they'd also be able to defend themselves against unfair accusations. It might even be a world where election administrators could start to build the professional norms essential to any well-functioning system.

As Opposed to What?

Perhaps the best reason to favor the Democracy Index returns us to a question I've asked repeatedly in this book: as opposed to what? You may not like the idea that voters use a ranking as a shorthand, but a well-designed ranking is better shorthand than what voters now use. You may think it's a bad idea for policymakers to rely on the Index as an information shortcut. But it's a better information shortcut than they have now. You might not like the idea that election administrators will be tempted to "teach to the test," but teaching to a well-designed test is better than having no test at all. As I noted in Chapter 4, it's easy to be against rankings in principle. It's only in practice that they start to look good. The "As opposed to what?" question also helps us assess whether creating a Democracy Index is worth its costs. I've tried to make the best case possible that an Index would work. Even if you don't buy everything I've said, it's worth asking yourself this question: As opposed to what? Is there a better reform proposal on the horizon?

I believe the answer is no. There are, of course, a plethora of reform proposals that could do a great deal of good in the world. But those proposals will not pass until we solve the here-to-there problem. The Index is a modest reform. But it's a modest reform that can make bigger, better reform possible. The Index beats out most alternatives for a simple reason: it should help make those alternatives possible.

Afterword

THE INVISIBLE ELECTION

The 2008 presidential election was one of those remarkable moments in politics when the nation was paying attention. The general election was hard fought, and the stakes could not have been higher. The storybook ending in Grant Park—where a black man accepted the presidency—was one that touched every American, from Obama's most ardent supporters to the people who accorded him the dignity of voting against him on the merits. I stood twenty feet away when Senator Obama became President-elect Obama. I watched as he pivoted from politician to president, as the paean to our history that had inspired Obama's supporters in New Hampshire became a sobering reminder of the enormous challenges the nation now faces. "Yes we can" was once a muscular chant invoked at partisan rallies. At Grant Park, it was quietly repeated by 100,000 people, as if it were part of a call-and-response between the president-elect and the nation, a secular amen.

The reason I was in Grant Park that night was that, as part of the campaign's election protection team, I had spent the previous nineteen hours working in the "boiler room," the spare office where ninety-six people ran the campaign's national election-day operations. As was typical of the notoriously thrifty campaign, the room was furnished cheaply and covered in industrial dust. Just after the networks called Ohio and everyone knew the race was over, the superstitious campaign staffers who had cried and cheered at the call suddenly scattered to find some genuine wood to knock on amidst the shoddy, plastic furniture.

While the furnishings were minimal, the campaign's election protection apparatus was well funded, precisely planned, and remarkably organized. Our goal was simple: to ensure that administrative slip-ups and partisan shenanigans did not prevent voters from casting a ballot and having that ballot counted. Over the course of the day, thousands of lawyers, campaign staff, and volunteers reported the problems they were seeing in polling places across the country. A sophisticated computer program allowed us to review these reports in real time so that we could assess whether and what corrective action needed to be taken.

What ran across my computer screen that day was the invisible election, the nuts-and-bolts details that journalists rarely report and citizens rarely see. Reports the day after claimed that the election had run smoothly, that there had been almost no problems, that we had dodged a bullet. In some jurisdictions, the reports were accurate. There were glitches, to be sure, but there were enough poll workers and election administrators to fix them as they came along.

In other jurisdictions, the reports bore no resemblance to what I saw scrolling across my computer screen. Many jurisdictions simply fell apart as wave after wave of voters crashed down upon them. Thousands of people had to wait three hours or more to vote. In some places, there weren't enough machines to process all the voters. In others, there were plenty of voting machines, but voting booths stood empty because there weren't enough poll workers to check people in. Machines broke down. Parking lots were full. Polling places were hard to find or had been moved at the last minute. Poll workers didn't know basic rules about provisional ballots and election protocols. Far too many people showed up at the polls thinking they had registered, only to be told they weren't on the rolls. A bewildering number of polling places needed pens by mid-day because theirs had run out of ink. Many polling places simply ran out of ballots.

These problems occurred even though more voters than ever before (an estimated third of the electorate) cast their ballots before Election Day. They occurred even though everyone knew that turnout would be extremely high. They occurred even though at least the Obama campaign—recognizing that victory depended on an election system capable of processing hundreds of thousands of new voters—had done an extraordinary amount of work in helping election administrators get ready for the turnout tsunami that was approaching.

What I saw in the boiler room was, in some ways, comforting. It seemed clear that most of the problems were caused not by partisan mischief, but by neglect—too little funding, too few resources devoted to planning, even something as simple as not enough poll workers showing up. It confirmed my view that we should never attribute to partisanship that which can be adequately explained by inadequate resources. It also became clear to me that it *is* possible to collect the data we need to build a Democracy Index. The Obama campaign was able to collect useful information on lines, registration problems, poll-worker mistakes, and machine breakdowns. There's no reason that state and localities, with adequate financial support and the help of nonprofit groups, can't do the same.

What matters most for our purposes, however, is this: these problems were all but invisible. They weren't reported anywhere, save a few media mentions of long lines. The reason, of course, is simple. The election wasn't close. The race didn't end up turning on the votes that were lost because people weren't properly registered or left the line in frustration. No one is going to investigate, let alone write a story about, problems that didn't affect the outcome. And even when social scientists get around to crunching the data, those data are so sparse that they will give us only a partial sense of what occurred.

Eight years have passed since the 2000 election transfixed the nation. Yet the same problems remain: long lines, registration problems, a dearth of poll workers, machine breakdowns. The same will be true for many elections to come unless we solve the "here to there" problem. The reason things haven't changed is that it's hard for reform to get traction in the United States. Until we change the reform environment—until we make election problems visible to voters and give politicians a reason to pay attention to them—we'll have to continue relying on the election administrator's prayer: "Lord, let this election not be close."

LOOKING TO THE FUTURE:

By the time this book goes to print in 2009, Barack Obama will have started his first term. Ask yourself what advice you would give him about next steps for improving our election system. I would urge our new president to start with the "here to there" problem and focus on creating an environment in which reform can actually get passed. Perhaps President

Obama will instantly be able to achieve what many have tried to do but failed, like creating national standards for administering elections or taking partisanship out of the process. But given how hard it is to get reform passed (and given that partisanship and localism can sometimes serve a useful role), my guess is that the first, realistic step toward reform is unlikely to involve proposals that would require partisan foxes to stop guarding the henhouse or our centuries-old tradition of localism to vanish overnight. Instead, the president should start by domesticating the foxes and harnessing the power of local competition. We may not have an ideal system in place. But we might as well take advantage of the best features of the current system—the powerful engine of partisanship and the intriguing possibilities associated with local competition. The Democracy Index does just that.

Were I offering advice, I'd tell our new president to start there . . . or, rather, to start with the "here to there." Given then-Senator Obama's decision to put the Democracy Index into proposed legislation, I suspect he already knows that. As he said on the Senate floor, the Index is "an important first step toward improving the health of our democracy" because it "will empower voters" and "encourage healthy competition among the states," helping us "work toward the goal we all share: an election system that makes us all proud."[1]

The Democracy Index is not the end of the reform process; it is the beginning. It's one of the best shots we have for creating an environment in which more far-reaching reform can take place. President-elect Obama is right. It's time to get started.

New Haven, Connecticut
November 15, 2008

Notes

INTRODUCTION: WHY WE NEED A DEMOCRACY INDEX

1. Abby Goodenough, "In Florida, Echoes of 2000 as Vote Questions Emerge," *New York Times*, November 10, 2006.

2. *Building Confidence in U.S. Elections: Report of the Federal Commission on Election Reform*, September 2005, available at http://american.edu/ia/cfer/.

3. Thad Hall et al., "Are Americans Confident Their Ballots Are Counted?" 3, unpublished draft, 2007.

4. Electionline, *Briefing: The 2006 Election*, 7 (2006), http://www.pewcenteronthestates.org/report_detail.aspx?id=32758.

5. Ariel J. Feldman, J. Alex Halderman, and Edward W. Felten, "Security Analysis of the Diebold AccuVote-TS Voting Machine," September 2006, http://itpolicy.princeton.edu/voting/summary.html.

6. Fred Hessler and Matt Smith, *City and County of Denver 2006 Election Technical and Operational Assessment*, December 8, 2006, 5, http://www.votetrustusa.org/pdfs/Colorado_Folder/Denver_Report.pdf.

7. Hessler and Smith, *Denver 2006 Election Technical and Operational Assessment.*

8. M. R. Kropko, "Election Staff Convicted in Recount Rig," washington.com, January 24, 2005.

9. "Ohio's Largest County Finishes Tabulating Votes Five Days after Primary," CantonRep.com, May 8, 2006; Dan Tokaji, "Cuyahoga County's Election Woes," Equal Vote Blog, May 9, 2006.

10. Press release, "Brunner Calls for Clean Slate in Cuyahoga County," http://www.sos.state.oh.us/.

11. Clive Thompson, "Can You Count on These Machines?" *New York Times Magazine*, January 6, 2008.

12. Joe Guillen, "20 Percent of Election Printouts Were Unreadable," *Cleveland Plain Dealer*, November 28, 2007; see also Thompson, "Can You Count on These Machines?"

13. Guillen, "20 Percent of Election Printouts."

14. The term was coined by Rick Hasen. See Richard L. Hasen, "Beyond the Margin of Litigation: Reforming Election Administration to Avoid Electoral Meltdown," 52 *Washington & Lee Law Review* 937 (2005).

15. Daniel P. Tokaji, "The Birth and Rebirth of Election Administration," 7 *Election Law Journal* 118, 121 (2007), reviewing Roy G. Saltman, *The History and Politics of Voting Technology: In Quest of Integrity and Public Confidence.*

16. Twenty percent of states do not report this information; they disclose only how many ballots were successfully counted. Thad Hall and Daniel Tokaji, "Money for Data: Funding the Oldest Unfunded Mandate," June 5, 2007, http://moritzlaw.osu.edu/blogs/tokaji/2007/06/money-for-data-funding-oldest-unfunded.html.

17. See, e.g., http://www.aclu.org/votingrights/exoffenders/statelegispolicy2007.html.

18. See, e.g., Chris Elmendorf, "Representation Reinforcement through Advisory Commissions: The Case of Election Law," 80 *New York University Law Review* 1366 (2005); Heather K. Gerken, "The Double-Edged Sword of Independence: Inoculating Electoral Reform Commissions against Everyday Politics," 6 *Election Law Journal* 184 (2007); Heather K. Gerken, "A Third Way for the Voting Rights Act: Section 5 and the Opt-in Approach," 106 *Columbia Law Review* 708 (2006); Heather K. Gerken, "Citizens Must Drive Electoral Reform," *Roll Call,* November 15, 2005; Heather Gerken and Chris Elmendorf, "Next Time, Start with the People," http://balkin.blogspot.com/2005/11/next-time-start-with-people.html; Michael Kang, "De-rigging Elections: Direct Democracy and the Future of Redistricting Reform," 84 *Washington University Law Review* 667 (2006); Dan Tokaji, "The Moneyball Approach to Election Reform," http://moritzlaw.osu.edu/electionlaw/comments/2005/051018.php.

19. I wrote about the "here to there" question in a series of blogs during the summer of 2007. See Heather K. Gerken, "A New Agenda for Election Law Scholarship," Balkinization, http://balkin.blogspot.com/ (series of posts dated June 18–22, 2007). At roughly the same time, political scientist Bruce Cain was writing about the need to create "a new sub-field of political reform" for an article that came out in *PS* in October, 2007. Bruce E. Cain, "Reform Studies: Political Science on the Firing Line," 15 *PS* 635, 635 (2007). Cain's focus is quite different from mine. The field he has in mind addresses reform writ large and includes existing work on redistricting, election administration, and campaign finance—the topics that make up the "there" part of the "here to there"

equation. Cain is absolutely right to emphasize the importance of pulling together these academic camps and doing a better job of integrating the normative, descriptive, and analytical components of our research. In my view, however, studying the reform process—the "here to there" problem—should be a subfield within the broad field of political reform that Cain proposes.

20. Carter-Baker Commission, *Building Confidence in U.S. Elections*, 25–26.

21. Interview with Justin Levitt, June 14, 2007.

22. There is, of course, an irony here. Funders are often reluctant to support projects like this one because it is hard to measure whether they are succeeding. As I note in chapter 2, however, one need not endorse the witless notion that everything can be measured to believe that election performance is susceptible to data-driven analysis.

CHAPTER 1: THE PERVERSE POLITICS OF ELECTION REFORM

1. These examples were all drawn from American Society of Civil Engineers' "Report Card for America's Infrastructure," which provides a state-by-state analysis of the problems associated with deferred maintenance, at http://www.asce.org/reportcard/2005/Index.cfm.

2. While most assumed at the time that deferred maintenance was the cause the Minnesota debacle, subsequent investigations suggest that a design problem led to the collapse. Matthew L. Wald, "Controversy Dogs Inquiry on Bridge Collapse," *New York Times*, January 30, 2008, 13.

3. The American Society of Civil Engineers estimates that we need to spend $1.6 trillion to "bring the nation's infrastructure to good condition." American Society of Civil Engineers, "Report Card for America's Infrastructure." The Government Performance Project gives the country a B− for its efforts to maintain our physical infrastructure. See http://www.pewcenteronthestates.org/gpp_report_card_details.aspx?id=35348.http://www.asce.org/reportcard/2005/index.cfm

4. For a useful survey of the problems associated with poll workers as well as a comparison of state training and compensation practices, see electionline.org, "Helping Americans Vote: Poll Workers," September 2007; Thad Hall and Quin Monson, "The Human Dimension of Elections: How Poll Workers Shape Public Confidence in Elections, 2007, unpublished draft, 3–4.

5. For useful surveys of the problems described in this paragraph, see, e.g., Caltech/MIT Voting Technology Project, "What Is, What Could Be," July 2001, www.votingtechnologyproject.org; Carter-Baker Commission, *Building Confidence in U.S. Elections*; General Accounting Office, "Elections: Perspectives on Activities and Challenges across the Nation," GAO-02-3, October 2001; Thad E. Hall and R. Michael Alvarez, "Why Everything That Can Go Wrong Often Does: An Analysis of Election Administration Problems," Caltech/MIT Voting Technology Project, VTP Working Paper 10, November 2003; Steven Huefner, Daniel P. Tokaji, and Edward B. Foley, *From Registration to Recounts: The Election Ecosystems of Five Midwestern States* (Columbus: Ohio State University Michael E. Moritz College of Law, 2007).

6. For initial research on making polling places more accessible, see J. G. Gimpel and J. E. Schuknecht, "Political Participation and the Accessibility of the Ballot Box," 22 *Political Geography* 471, 471 (2003); Moshe Haspel and H. Gibbs Knotts, "Location, Location, Location: Precinct Placement and the Costs of Voting," 67 *Journal of Politics* 560, 561 (2005); Robert M. Stein and Greg Vonnahme, "Election Day Voter Centers and Voter Turnout," unpublished manuscript, 2006; Robert M. Stein and Patricia A. Garcia-Monet, "Voting Early but Not Often," 78 *Social Science Quarterly* 657 (1997).

7. I draw these statistics from estimates offered in Alan Agresti and Brett Presnell, "Misvotes, Undervotes, and Overvotes: The 2000 Presidential Election in Florida," 17 *Statistical Science* 436 (2002), and the U.S. Commission on Civil Rights, *Voting Irregularities in Florida during the 2000 Presidential Election* (Washington, D.C.: Government Printing Office, 2001). More detailed accounts of these events can be found in the large number of books on the subject, including Ronald Dworkin, ed., *A Badly Flawed Election: Debating Bush v. Gore, the Supreme Court, and American Democracy* (New York: New Press, 2002); Bruce Ackerman, ed., *Bush v. Gore: The Question of Legitimacy* (New Haven: Yale University Press, 2002); Arthur Jacobson and Michael Rosenfeld, eds., *The Longest Night: Polemics and Perspectives on Election 2000* (Berkeley and Los Angeles: University of California Press, 2002); Richard A. Posner, *Breaking the Deadlock: The 2000 Election, the Constitution, and the Courts* (Princeton, N.J.: Princeton University Press, 2001); Jack Rakove, ed., *The Unfinished Election of 2000* (New York: Basic Books, 2001); and Cass R. Sunstein and Richard A. Epstein, eds., *The Vote: Bush, Gore, and the Supreme Court* (Chicago: University of Chicago Press, 2001).

8. Richard Hasen, "Voting System Is Haunted by Democratic Meltdown, *Canberra Times*, January 22, 2008.

9. Caltech/MIT Voting Project, "What Is, What Could Be," 8.

10. Caltech/MIT Voting Technology Project, "Immediate Steps to Avoid Lost Votes in the 2004 Presidential Election: Recommendations for the Election Assistance Commission," 2004, 3.

11. Carter-Baker Commission, *Building Confidence in U.S. Elections*, 54.

12. Eric A. Fischer and Kevin J. Coleman, *Election Reform and Local Election Officials: Results of Two National Surveys*, Congressional Research Service Report for Congress, RL-34363, February 7, 2008.

13. See http://www.washingtonpost.com/wp-dyn/politics/elections/2004/ for state-by-state election results for 2004 presidential race.

14. Richard Lacayo, "Eye of the Storm," *Time*, November 20, 2000.

15. See, e.g., Timothy Egan, "Questions Linger as Governor Takes Over Washington," *New York Times*, January 13, 2005, A20; Mike Francher, "Governor's Race to Make Many Voters Feel Cheated," *Seattle Times*, December 26, 2004; Sarah Kershaw, "Governor-Elect Declared in Washington Recounts," *New York Times*, December 31, 2006, A18.

16. Roy G. Saltman, *The History and Politics of Voting Technology: In Quest of Integrity and Public Confidence* (New York: Palgrave Macmillan, 2006), 185.

17. For a granular analysis of changes since 2000 and the effects of HAVA, see electionline.org, "Election Reform: What's Changed, What Hasn't and Why," November 2006; electionline.org, "The Help America Vote Act," 2007, 5.

18. Deborah Hastings, "Problems, Funding Plague Voting Panel," Associated Press, June 23, 2008.

19. See, e.g., Norm Ornstein, "Voting Machine Mess Can't Just Be Fixed by Congressional Bilks," *Roll Call*, November 26, 2007.

20. Feldman, Halderman, and Felten, "Security Analysis."

21. As the Carter-Baker Commission has observed, "Most other democratic countries have found ways to insulate election administration from politics and partisanship by establishing truly autonomous, professional, and nonpartisan independent national election commissions that function almost like a fourth branch of government" (*Building Confidence in U.S. Elections*, 49). For helpful comparative surveys, see Michael Gallagher and Paul Mitchell, eds., *The Politics of Electoral Systems* (New York: Oxford University Press, 2005); Louis Massicotte, Andreï Blais, and Antoine Yoshinaka, *Establishing the Rules of the Game: Election*

Laws in Democracies (Toronto: University of Toronto Press, 2004); Administration and Cost of Elections Project Survey, http://aceproject.org/.

22. For instance, most secretaries of state are elected, and many subsidiary election positions, such as membership on election boards, are either elected or awarded based on partisan affiliation. See Hasen, "Beyond the Margin of Litigation," 974.

23. Compare Samuel Issacharoff, "Gerrymandering and Political Cartels," 116 *Harvard Law Review* 593 (2002), with Nathan Persily, "In Defense of Foxes Guarding Henhouses: The Case for Judicial Acquiescence to Incumbent-Protecting Gerrymanders," 116 *Harvard Law Review* 649 (2002).

24. Interview with Chris Nelson, January 25, 2008.

25. Huefner, Tokaji, and Foley, *From Registration to Recounts*, 170; see also David C. Kimball, Martha Kropf, and Lindsay Battles, "Helping America Vote? Election Administration, Partisanship, and Provisional Voting in the 2004 Election," 5 *Election Law Journal* 447 (2006), which finds some evidence that partisanship influenced choices on provisional balloting rules.

26. Dan Tokaji, "The New Vote Denial: Where Election Reform Meets the Voting Rights Act," 57 *South Carolina Law Review* 689 (2006).

27. The facts in this paragraph and the next are drawn from Huefner, Tokaji, and Foley, *From Registration to Recounts*, chap. 3; Laura A. Bischoff, "Blackwell Plays Pivotal Role in Elections, *Dayton Daily News*, October 4, 2004, 1A; Joe Hallette, "Campaign Consequences: Blackwell Faces Own Referendum on Election Day," *Columbus Dispatch*, October 19, 2004, 1A.

28. Interview with Trey Grayson, January 9, 2008.

29. Grayson, interview.

30. Interview with Conny McCormack, October 26, 2007.

31. McCormack argues that there are "professional politicians" at the top and "professional administrators" at the bottom of the election administration hierarchy (McCormack, interview).

32. Robert Bauer, "Partisanship and the Dark Side of Election Law," http://www.moresoftmoneyhardlaw.com/.

33. Interview with Joe Mansky, June 6, 2008.

34. Tokaji, "Birth and Rebirth," 121.

35. Saltman, *History and Politics*, 185.

36. Kimball Brace, testimony before the Committee on House Administration, April 15, 2008.

37. What follows is drawn from an interview conducted on June 23, 2008, and a handout Streater authored entitled "Duties of a County Clerk."

38. Fischer and Coleman, "Election Reform."

39. Fischer and Coleman, "Election Reform," 2–3, 6.

40. Fischer and Coleman, "Election Reform," 6.

41. Fischer and Coleman, "Election Reform," 31.

42. Except where indicated, the quotations and information in the next three paragraphs are drawn from an interview with Gary Smith on May 21, 2008.

43. "GEOA Wage and Benefit Survey—2005" (on file with the author).

44. Pew Election 2008 Forum, Washington, D.C., December 10, 2007.

45. Interview with Matthew Damschroder, October 29, 2007.

46. Or, perhaps more accurately, in elections we see a race to get as close to the bottom as one can get without the entire system breaking down.

47. Grayson, interview.

48. Grayson, interview.

49. Interview with Jennifer Brunner, January 28, 2008.

50. The problem, of course, is that a standard with wiggle room will invite reformers to shoehorn their favorite causes into the Index. Many reformers are convinced that if they had a chance to sit down with everyday citizens, they could persuade them of the importance of reforming campaign finance or re-enfranchising felons. We are likely to see a push from parts of the reform community to expand the Democracy Index to measure not just the performance of election administrators, but the democratic health of the state itself. They may want to rank states low for disenfranchising felons or failing to make affirmative efforts to overcome the effects of poverty on participation rates. Reformers will argue, with some justification, that some of what I want to exclude from the Index could properly be classified as mismanagement, or at least a departure from internationally defined best practices.

Though I am deeply sympathetic to these arguments, let me make the case for restraint. If the Index is going to influence voters and policymakers, it must be perceived as a straight-down-the-middle, nonpartisan effort to measure how election systems perform. It will be too easy to deflect politically if it becomes yet another laundry list of reformers' (liberal) pet projects. Supporters of the Index will spend all of their time arguing about the morality of felon disenfranchisement or the sociology of poverty rather than whether ballots are being counted properly. To the election administrators in poor states whose buy-in is essential for the Index to work, it will seem that they have to do more than others to achieve the same score, that the Index measures luck, not skill. Remedying these bigger problems is important, but the Index is not the right tool to fix them.

51. The line between a policy input and a performance output can be fuzzy. For instance, a badly maintained registration list might be classified as a performance output, the result of a poor data-entry system. Or it might be thought of as a policy input in the voting process, one that will result in voters being turned away from the polls on Election Day.

52. I am indebted to Cameron Quinn, the chief elections officer under Virginia governor Jim Gilmore, for pushing me on these issues.

53. David Roodman, "Building and Running an Effective Policy Index: Lessons from the Commitment to Development Index," March 2006, available at http://www.cgdev.org/content/publications/detail/6661.

54. Roodman, "Building and Running an Index," 7.

55. Roodman, "Building and Running an Index," 12.

56. Charles Stewart III, "Residual Vote in the 2004 Election," 5 *Election Law Journal* 158 (2006).

57. Stephen Ansolabehere and Charles Steward II, "Residual Vote Rates Attributable to Technology," 67 *Journal of Politics* 365, 366 (2005).

58. Let me expand on each of these points. During the early stages of development, redundancy provides a safety net that helps us gauge whether each of the metrics is working. For instance, if the metrics don't rise and fall together, that should tell us something useful about whether they are measuring the same thing. Even setting aside the problem of uncertainty, a comprehensive set of metrics will make it harder for a jurisdiction to improve its standing by focusing on one or two problems and neglecting the rest of its duties. Any effort to divert resources to one metric will likely have ripple effects on other parts of the jurisdiction's scorecard. Moreover, trade-offs are inevitable in election reform; a change in one part of the system can cause problems elsewhere. We need to be confident that both the costs and the benefits of any trade-offs are captured in the Index, lest jurisdictions adopt policies that generate modest gains for something included in the Index while creating problems in an areas not measured by the Index. Finally, comprehensive metrics should provide a useful backstop against cheating. Multiple measurement strategies make it harder for jurisdictions to game the numbers. This strategy is particularly important when we are

relying on jurisdictions to report their own data. Having at least one rough proxy from another source helps us figure out whether someone is cooking the books.

59. Presentation of Lynn Olson, Designing a Democracy Index Conference, September 28, 2007.

60. Charles Stewart III, "Measuring the Improvement (or Lack of Improvement) in Voting since 2000 in the U.S.," Caltech/MIT Voting Technology Project, VTP Working Paper 36, August 2005, 7.

61. See chapter 4.

62. Any effort at standardization will also require some statistical work. For instance, designers of the Index will have to figure out what to do with the raw data in order to compare numbers across states. Does one rank the states 1–50 for each metric and then add up their rankings within a given category? Follow the example of the Environmental Performance Index and use a "proximity-to-target" approach, which estimates how close each state gets to the performance target in each area? For the EPI approach, see Yale Center for Environmental Law and Policy, Yale University, and Center for International Earth Science Information Network (CIESIN), Columbia University, *Pilot 2006 Environmental Performance Index Report*, 281, http://www.yale.edu/epi/2006EPI_Report_Full.pdf. Similarly, designers of the Index must figure out what to do with data that fall at the tail end of the distribution. The danger is that a score in one category may be so low as to swamp all of the remaining categories when they are added together. Statistical techniques are necessary to be sure you hold a state accountable for an unusually low score without making the entire Index turn on that score. The designers of the EPI, for instance, "winsorize" the lowest fifth percentile of the data; anything that falls below the fifth percentile mark is automatically converted to the value that corresponds to the fifth percentile (*EPI Report*, 281).

63. Interview with Dan Esty, October 24, 2007; Roodman, "Building and Running an Index," 5; see also chapter 4 in this book. For instance, Philip Joyce, who has been involved in putting together the Government Performance Project, argues that the GPP could not use a single, composite ranking because it "implies a level of specificity that the data don't really back up" (interview with Philip Joyce, September 19, 2007). Another reason not to provide a single, composite ranking is that you believe the categories involved are sufficiently distinct that you want to reward a state for doing well in one area even if it falls short in another. This is the justification for the Quality Counts approach, which gives

states letter grades in six areas but refuses to provide a single ranking (Olson, presentation at Designing a Democracy Index Conference).

64. Roodman, "Building and Running an Index."

CHAPTER 2: THE PROMISE OF DATA-DRIVEN REFORM

1. What follows below is drawn from Spencer Overton's published dissent to the Carter-Baker Commission, "Dissenting Statement," http://www.carter bakerdissent.com/dissent.php; an article he wrote on the controversy, "Voter Identification," 105 *Michigan Law Review* 631 (2007); and two phone interviews. Direct quotations are attributed to the specific source in each instance.

2. Spencer Overton, *Stealing Democracy: The New Politics of Voter Suppression* (New York: Norton, 2006).

3. Interview with Spencer Overton, November 15, 2007.

4. Carter-Baker Commission, *Building Confidence in U.S. Elections.*

5. Carter-Baker Commission, *Building Confidence in U.S. Elections,* 18.

6. Stephen Ansolabehere and Nathan Persily, "Voter Fraud in the Eye of the Beholder: The Role of Public Opinion in the Challenge to Voter Identification Requirements," 121 *Harvard Law Review* 1737 (2008).

7. Overton, "Voter Identification," 634.

8. Overton, "Dissenting Statement."

9. On the one hand, as Overton observed, his numbers might lead one to overestimate the effect of an identification requirement. For example, voters who don't possess ID may "have lower participation rates," so that an identification requirement may not have a significant effect on turnout (Overton, "Voter Identification," 660). Moreover, people who do not currently possess an ID might try to get one rather than sit out an election ("Voter Identification," 661). On the other hand, Overton's numbers may underestimate the effect of an identification requirement. For instance, even people who possess ID might be deterred from voting because of the hassle involved in bringing it to the polls. ("Voter Identification," 661).

10. Overton, "Voter Identification," 636.

11. Overton, "Voter Identification," 635.

12. Overton, interview.

13. *Crawford v. Marion County Election Board,* 472 F.3d 949, 954 (2007) (Evans, J., dissenting).

14. *Crawford v. Marion County Election Bd.*, 128 S. Ct. 1610 (2008).

15. Lev Tolstoy, as translated by Diego Gambetta in "'Claro! An Essay on Discursive Machismo," in *Deliberative Democracy*, ed. Jon Elster (New York: Cambridge University Press, 1998), 19.

16. Hall and Tokaji, "Money for Data."

17. Cal Tech/MIT Voting Technology Project, "Insuring the Integrity of the Election Process: Recommendations for Consistent and Complete Reporting of Election Data," October 2004.

18. Stewart, "Measuring the Improvement," 35.

19. Hall and Tokaji, "Money for Data." The difference between absentee and early ballots is complicated. If you are ever at an election administration cocktail party and don't know what to say, just raise the question, step back, and enjoy your martini.

20. Carter-Baker Commission, *Building Confidence in U.S. Elections*, 57.

21. Election Assistance Commission, *2006 Election Administration and Voting Survey*, http://www.eac.gov/News/press/clearinghouse/2006-election-administration-and-voting-survey.

22. 42 U.S.C. § 15322.

23. The three reports that the EAC published on election administration are *2006 Election Administration and Voting Survey, 2005–2006 National Voter Registration Act Survey*, and *2006 Uniformed and Overseas Citizen Voting Act*, all available at http://www.eac.gov/clearinghouse/reports-and-surveys/.

24. Many thanks to Peter Miller for his work in creating this ranking and to the folks at the Pew Center on the States and electionline.org for suggesting the idea in the first place. For a full view of the scoring prior to aggregation, see democracyindex.com.

25. These included (1) the numbers of active and inactive voters, (2) the number of voters registered on Election Day (for the states that allow for Election Day registration), (3) the manner and location voters were registered, (4) the number of registrations rejected and the reasons for the rejection, (5) the number of registrations removed and reasons for the removal, (6) the number of ballots cast and counted, (7) reasons for rejecting provisional ballots, (8) the reasons for rejecting domestic absentee ballots, (9) the number of undervotes and overvotes, (10) information regarding the number of precincts and polling places, poll worker information, and information regarding the accessibility of polling places for people with disabilities, (11) the number of ballots cast and counted

from voters covered by UOCAVA (overseas voters, domestic military voters, and overseas civilian voters), (12) the number of absentee ballots sent and received under UOCAVA, (13) the number of UOCAVA ballots that were rejected. These categories correspond to the data categories in each report. Because the jurisdiction count was unavailable for overvote and undervote reporting below the state level, this category was excluded from the ranking.

26. A state that reported 100 percent of its data in a given category was awarded a 1. A state that reported all of the data requested for only half of its jurisdictions would receive a 0.5 in that category. For a state like Alaska, which reports only at the state level, the state was treated as a single jurisdiction. So, too, a state that reported half of the data requested for all of its jurisdictions would receive a 0.5 in that category as well.

27. For instance, localities that reported a 0 in a given category (rather than leaving it blank) were counted as properly reporting their data even when it was difficult to believe that the score represents an accurate report. As noted in the text, several states reported that there were zero votes were cast by overseas military voters. Further, as noted above, because the jurisdiction count was unavailable for overvotes and undervotes reporting below the state level, this category was excluded from the ranking.

28. Alabama, for instance, tended to have high reporting rates for some portions of each survey but quite low reporting rates for others, resulting in a very low overall ranking. Similarly, Vermont provided complete or near-complete data for basic questions (e.g., how many provisional ballots or absentee ballots were rejected) but failed to report data on the reasons why these ballots were rejected. While the latter information is important for reasons I outline below, Vermont at least had good data on the primary questions.

29.. For the full table, see democracyindex.com.

30. The information in this and the next paragraph was provided by Peter Miller, who played a significant role in pulling the EAC study together.

31. Carter-Baker Commission, *Building Confidence in U.S. Elections*, 54.

32. Ian Ayres, *Super Crunchers: Why Thinking-by-Numbers Is the New Way to Be Smart* (New York: Bantam, 2007).

33. Emily Nelson, "Retailing: Why Wal-Mart Sings, 'Yes, We Have Bananas!'" *Wall Street Journal*, October 6, 1998, B1.

34. Constance L. Hays, "What Wal-Mart Knows about Customers' Habits," *New York Times*, November 14, 2005.

35. "Priority Is Clear: Improve the Shopping Experience," *MMR*, December 11, 2006, 53.

36. See, e.g., Brennan Center for Justice, *The Machinery of Democracy: Voting System Security, Accessibility, Usability, and Cost*, 2006, http://brennan.3cdn.net/cb325689a9bbe2930e_0am6b09p4.pdf.

37. Stewart, "Measuring the Improvement," 23 ("The best data we have to track how the use of voting machines is evolving is still imprecise and incomplete").

38. See, e.g., Julia Melkers and Katherine Willoughby, *Staying the Course: The Use of Performance Measurements in State Governments*, IBM Center for Business and Government, November 2004, http://www.businessofgovernment.org/pdfs/MelkersReport.pdf.

39. For a survey, see Harry P. Hatry, Elaine Morley, Shelli B. Rossman, and Joseph S. Wholey, *How Federal Programs Use Outcome Information: Opportunities for Federal Managers*, IBM Center for Business and Government, May 2003, http://www.businessofgovernment.org/pdfs/HatryReport.pdf.

40. For a useful sampling of these programs, see Daniel C. Esty and Reece Rushing, *Governing by the Numbers: The Promise of Data-Driven Policymaking in the Information Age*, April 23, 2007, http://www.americanprogress.org/issues/2007/04/data_driven_policy.html.

41. See, e.g., Paul O'Connell, *Using Performance Data for Accountability: The New York City Police Department's CompStat Model of Police Management*, IBM Center for Business and Government, August 2001, http://www.businessofgovernment.org/pdfs/Oconnell_Report.pdf.

42. For a comprehensive but perhaps unduly cheerful analysis of CitiStat, see Robert D. Behn, *What All Mayors Would Like to Know about Baltimore's CitiStat Performance Strategy*, IBM Center for Business and Government, 2007, http://www.businessofgovernment.org/pdfs/BehnReportCiti.pdf.

43. Behn, *What All Mayors Would Like to Know*, 9.

44. O'Connell, *Using Performance Data for Accountability*.

45. Hatry et al., *How Federal Programs Use Outcome Information*, 37–43.

46. Hatry et al., *How Federal Programs Use Outcome Information*, 57–58.

47. Hatry et al., *How Federal Programs Use Outcome Information*, 21–30.

48. Charles P. Kindleberger, *Manias, Panics, and Crashes: A History of Financial Crises*, 4th ed. (New York: Wiley, 2000), 105.

49. Federal Agencies with Statistical Programs, http://www.fedstats.gov/agencies/.

50. The facts in this section were drawn from interviews I conducted with Esty as well as his writings. Direct quotations from those interviews and his writings are cited individually.

51. Daniel Esty, *Greening the GATT: Trade, Environment, and the Future* (Washington, D.C.: Institute for International Economics, 1994).

52. Esty, interview.

53. The report is available at http://www.weforum.org/en/initiatives/gcp/Global%20Competitiveness%20Report/Index.htm.

54. Dan Esty, presentation at Designing a Democracy Index Conference, Columbus, Ohio, September 29, 2007.

55. The ranking and information on its constructions is available at http://www.yale.edu/epi/.

56. See http://sedac.ciesin.columbia.edu/es/esi/rank_01.html.

57. http://www.yale.edu/epi/.

58. Esty, presentation at Designing a Democracy Index Conference.

59. http://www.carbonfootprint.com/.

60. Esty, interview.

61. Esty, interview.

62. Esty, interview.

63. Esty, interview.

64. Tokaji, "Moneyball Approach."

65. Roger Angell, *Once More around the Park: A Baseball Reader* (New York: Ballantine, 1991), 4. Many thanks to Doug Chapin for sharing this with me.

66. Michael Lewis, *Moneyball: The Art of Winning an Unfair Game* (New York: Norton, 2003).

67. Tokaji, "Moneyball Approach."

68. Tokaji, "Moneyball Approach."

69. Tokaji, "Moneyball Approach."

70. The information in this paragraph is all drawn from an interview with Bob Murphy, July 8, 2008.

71. Smith, interview.

72. Gary Smith, "Using GIS Data to Confirm Viability of Early Voting Sites," http://datafordemocracy.org/blog/?q=node/17.

73. Interview with Joe Mansky, May 6, 2008.

74. Huefner, Tokaji, and Foley, *From Registration to Recounts*, v.

75. Some initial answers to these questions have been offered by a group of scholars based on an in-depth, qualitative study of five election systems in the Midwest (Huefner, Tokaji, and Foley, *From Registration to Recounts*). This important study should be immensely useful in trying to figure out how to generate answers to these questions on a larger scale once better data becomes available.

76. *New State Ice Co. v. Liebmann*, 285 U.S. 262, 311 (1932) (Brandeis, J., dissenting). Scholars of "democratic experimentalism" have explored the practical and theoretical dimensions of benchmarking in the governance context. See, e.g., Joshua Cohen and Charles Sabel, "Directly-Deliberative Polyarchy," 3 *European Law Journal* 313 (1997); Michael Dorf and Charles F. Sabel, "A Constitution of Democratic Experimentalism," 98 *Columbia Law Review* 267 (1988).

CHAPTER 3: THE POLITICS OF REFORM AND THE PROMISE OF RANKING

1. Public choice scholars would not be surprised that an issue that affects everyone is not at the forefront of the political agenda. Oddly enough, minority groups—sometimes condemned as "special interests"—are often the ones that succeed best in a majoritarian system like our own. See, e.g., Bruce Ackerman, "Beyond *Carolene Products*," 98 *Harvard Law Review* 713 (1985). Political scientist Robert Dahl famously claimed that "minorities rule" in the United States; coalitions of organized interest groups join together to form majorities and get legislation passed. Robert Dahl, *A Preface to Democratic Theory* (Chicago: University of Chicago Press, 1956), 133. Or, as Jesse Jackson put it, "In politics, an organized minority is a political majority" (CNN, *Both Sides with Jesse Jackson*, Transcript 0013000V49, January 30, 2000). What matters in a system where "minorities rule" is the ability to organize—to turn out the vote, lobby representatives, and raise money. And it is often easier to organize a small, easily identified group with a concrete complaint than it is to get a large majority affected by a diffuse harm to coalesce. The public choice explanation is not, of course, a complete answer. Other problems that impose diffuse harms are salient to voters and thus to politicians. For instance, politicians are careful to sketch out positions on things like the environment or foreign policy. Moreover, politicians are notoriously risk averse; none of them is going to be enthusiastic about

flouting the preferences of the majority even when no special interest group is there to fight about it.

2. Building on the work of Erving Goffman in *Frame Analysis: An Essay on the Organization of Experience* (New York: Harper and Row, 1974), social scientists have extensively analyzed the ways that issues are presented to, and affect the behavior of, voters. For a sampling of this literature, see Frank R. Baumgartner and Bryan D. Jones, *Agendas and Instability in American Politics* (Chicago: University of Chicago Press, 1993); Dennis Chong and James N. Druckman, "Framing Theory," 10 *American Review of Political Science* 103 (2007); James N. Druckman, "Political Preference Formation: Competition, Deliberation, and the (Ir)relevance of Framing Effects," 98 *American Political Science Review* 671 (2004); Shanto Iyengar and Donald Kinder, *News That Matters: Television and American Opinion* (Chicago: University of Chicago Press, 1987); William H. Riker, *The Art of Political Manipulation* (New Haven: Yale University Press, 1986); Deborah A. Stone, *Policy Paradox and Political Reason* (Glenview, Ill.: Scott, Foresman, 1988); Deborah A. Stone, "Causal Stories and the Formation of Policy Agendas," 104 *Political Science Quarterly* 281 (1989).

3. Interview with Jonah Goldman, January 4, 2008.

4. Lest you think that only a law professor would feel the need to footnote this claim, it is worth noting that many scholars argue, with some evidence, that voters cast their ballots in an irrational fashion. See, e.g., Bryan Caplan, *The Myth of the Rational Voter: Why Democracies Choose Bad Policies* (Princeton, N.J.: Princeton University Press, 2007). Arguments like these often underestimate the useful role that heuristics can play in guiding voting behavior, a point nicely made by David Schleicher in his review of Caplan's book in "Irrational Voters, Rational Voting," 7 *Election Law Journal* 149.

5. Take a look at the fights that recently took place over redistricting reform in Ohio and California. Rightly or wrongly, those were precisely the kinds of accusations levied against those trying to prevent legislators from drawing their own districts. In Ohio, for instance, critics of the initiative repeatedly branded it a Democratic power grab. See, e.g., "Case against Issue 4 Takes a Hit," *Dayton Daily News*, November 3, 2005, at A14 ("From the beginning of the debate about Issue 4, critics have portrayed it as a Democratic effort to take power from Republicans"); Kevin O'Brien, "Reform Ohio Now? No, No, and No," *Cleveland Plain Dealer*, October 19, 2005, B11 ("It's easy to see why Republicans don't want to see Ohio change the rules that govern political fund-raising, leg-

islative district mapping, elections supervision and political fund-raising. They hold all of the high cards at the moment. . . . It's just as easy to see why the Democrats are dying to change the rules. They're so short of high cards, they've practically been dealt out of the game").

6. Aha. I knew you'd be curious enough to peek at the note. See http://www.natives.co.uk/news/2002/0502/08iron.htm.

7. See http://www.usarps.com/Index.php. I should emphasize here that I side with Demetri Martin, who is flummoxed as to why paper can beat rock just by covering it. He proposes instead that the game should be called, "rock, dynamite with a cuttable wick, scissors" (http://www.devilducky.com/media/79750/).

8. See http://www.westmountgolf.com/mcindex.htm.

9. A recent study reveals that two of five voters surveyed stated that "they could not evaluate their local election administrator." Lonna R. Atkeson and Kyle L. Saunders, "The Effect of Election Administration on Voter Confidence: A Local Matter?" 15 *PS* 655, 659 (2007).

10. Esty, interview.

11. See, e.g., Samuel L. Popkin, *The Reasoning Voter: Communication and Persuasion in Presidential Campaigns*, 2nd ed. (Chicago: University of Chicago Press, 1994).

12. For early work in what is now a vast literature, see, e.g., John H. Aldrich, *Why Parties? The Origin and Transformation of Political Parties in America* (Chicago: University of Chicago Press, 1995); Bernard R. Berelson, Paul F. Lazarsfeld, and William N. McPhee, *Voting: A Study of Opinion Formation in Presidential Campaigns* (Chicago: University of Chicago Press, 1954); Angus Campbell, Philip E. Converse, Warren E. Miller, and Donald E. Stokes, *The American Voter* (New York: Wiley, 1960); V. O. Key, Jr. and Frank Munger, "Social Determinism and Electoral Decisions: The Case of Indiana," in *American Voting Behavior*, ed. Eugene Burdick and Arthur J. Brodbeck (Glencoe, Ill.: Free Press, 1959).

13. See, e.g., Richard R. Lau and David P. Redlawski, "Voting Correctly," 91 *American Political Science Review* 585, 590 (1997); Arthur Lupia, "Shortcuts versus Encyclopedias: Information and Voting Behavior in California Insurance Reform Elections," 88 *American Political Science Review* 63 (1994); Arthur Lupia, "Dumber Than Chimps? An Assessment of Direct Democracy Voters," in *Dangerous Democracy? The Battle over Ballot Initiatives in American*, ed. Larry Sabato, Howard R. Ernst, and Bruce A. Larson (Lanham, Md.: Rowman and Littlefield, 2001); Popkin, *The Reasoning Voter.*

14. Berelson, Lazarsfeld, and McPhee, *Voting*, 321.

15. Indeed, a major movement within political science insists that we need strong, cohesive parties in order to give voters a better predictive cue as to how candidates will vote. Better party cues, the argument goes, means greater accountability. This notion of "responsible party government" was first endorsed by the American Political Science Association's Committee on Political Parties in 1950. See American Political Science Association, "Toward a More Responsible Two-Party System: A Report of the Committee on Political Parties," 44 *American Political Science Review* (Supp. Sept. 1950).

16. This sentence oversimplifies things a bit. As I have noted, whether the Democracy Index gets traction will depend on what is happening in the political arena.

17. News release, Office of Governor Chris Gregoire, "Washington Earns Top Rating for Managing Public Resources," March 3, 2008; news release, "Virginia Gets Top Grade in Performance," March 3, 2008.

18. See, e.g., David Schleicher, "Why Is There No Partisan Competition in Local Elections? The Role of Election Law," 23 *Journal of Law and Politics* 419 (2008).

19. I am indebted to David Schleicher, whose work on the role of partisan heuristics in local elections suggested this line of criticism and whose conversation helped me work out a response.

20. Michael S. Kang, "The Hydraulics of Politics and Party Regulation," 91 *Iowa Law Review* 131, 151 (2005).

21. Thanks to an anonymous reviewer for suggesting this line of critique.

22. Caltech/MIT Voting Technology Project, "Insuring the Integrity."

23. Caltech/MIT Voting Technology Project, "Insuring the Integrity."

24. Press release, "Brennan Center Report Finds New Improvements in New Voting Technology Being Implemented in Several States," http://www.brennancenter.org/content/resource/brennan_center_report_finds_improvements_in_new_voting_technology_being_imp.

25. Government Performance Project: "About Us," http://www.gpponline.org/AboutUs.aspx.

26. Unless otherwise noted, what follows in the next two paragraphs is drawn from an interview with Richard Greene conducted on June 12, 2008.

27. David S. Broder, "Managing: An Affair of States," *Washington Post*, March 9, 2008, B7.

28. Pew Center for the States, Government Performance Project, http://www.pewcenteronthestates.org/states_overview.aspx?abrv=GA.

29. http://sedac.ciesin.columbia.edu/es/esi/rank_01.html.

30. Esty, interview.

31. For a survey of this literature, see the section "Can the Democracy Index Help?" in this chapter.

32. Interview with Cameron Quinn, December 21, 2007.

33. http://www.imdb.com/title/tt0417433/quotes. Many thanks to David Pervin for suggesting the reference.

34. Levitt, interview.

35. Thanks to an anonymous reviewer for offering this critique.

36. E. E. Schattschneider, *The Semisovereign People: A Realist's View of Democracy in America* (New York: Holt, Rinehart and Winston, 1960), 68.

37. See the works cited in note 2 to this chapter.

38. Goldman, interview. For an excellent overview of the role of framing in this debate, see R. Michael Alvarez and Thad E. Hall, *Electronic Elections: The Perils and Promises of Digital Democracy* (Princeton, N.J.: Princeton University Press, 2008).

39. See, e.g., Daniel Tokaji, "The Paperless Trail: Electronic Voting and Democratic Values," 73 *Fordham Law Review* 1711 (2005).

40. See, e.g., HR 811 (the "Holt bill").

41. Political competition represents an important force in shaping public opinion. As Robert Bennett explains, "American democracy is an extraordinary engine for producing a conversation about democratic affairs" that ultimately shapes "the content of public policy decisions." Robert W. Bennett, *Talking It Through: Puzzles of American Democracy* (Ithaca, N.Y.: Cornell University Press, 2003), 2. The fuel for that engine is political competition, as political leaders compete against one another to "shape, coordinate, and frame the public's understanding about electoral politics, public policy, and civic affairs." Michael Kang, "Race and Democratic Contestation," *Yale Law Journal*, forthcoming, draft at 15–16. The literature on the relationship between political competition and public opinion dates back at least to the work of venerable political scientists like V. O. Key and Schattschneider. See, e.g., V. O. Key, *The Responsible Electorate: Rationality in Presidential Voting, 1936–1960* (Cambridge: Belknap Press of Harvard University Press, 1966); and Schattschneider, *The Semisovereign People*. Scholars often call these leaders "political entrepreneurs" because of the

creative ways in which they forge new platforms, frame issues, and exploit latent political energies in the process of building new political coalitions. See, e.g., Kang, "Race and Democratic Contestation," 4 n. 17. For a necessarily incomplete sampling of the seminal work in this area, see William H. Riker, *The Strategy of Rhetoric: Campaigning for the American Constitution*, ed. Randall L. Calvert, John Mueller, and Rick K. Wilson (New Haven: Yale University Press, 1996); Schattschneider, *The Semisovereign People*; Key; *The Responsible Electorate*; Roger W. Cobb and Charles D. Elder, *Participation in American Politics: The Dynamics of Agenda-Building* (Boston: Allyn and Bacon, 1972).

42. One could, of course, make an argument like this about most "latent" reform platforms that are amenable to effective framing. But few issues are as closely linked to partisan politics as this one. We are *already* waging political battles in which the Index could be used as a partisan weapon.

43. http://eirs.cs.net:8080/EIRS_WEB/User/findHome.do.

44. Stewart, "Measuring the Improvement," 16.

45. Goldman, interview.

46. Goldman, interview.

47. Anonymous interview, April 15, 2008.

48. Presentation of Lynn Olson, Designing a Democracy Index Conference, September 28, 2007.

49. Joyce, interview.

50. Grayson, interview.

51. Pew Journalists Forum, December 10, 2007.

52. As Bruce Cain observes:

> [T]he real effects of reform are usually smaller in every direction . . . mainly because of their intermingling with other factors that work in the opposite direction. . . . Because reform is usually made in a politically charged setting, the claims and counter-claims of opposing sides are often exaggerated and simplistic. Campaign finance reformers, for example, often imply that a proposed change will lessen corruption or lower election costs. Redistricting changes promise neutral and fair procedures, or higher levels of competition. New voting technology was supposed to end voter confusion and restore confidence in the election process. . . . In fact, the claims on both sides rarely live up to the hype. ("Reform Studies," 637)

53. Doug Caruso, "Vendor's Donation Questioned," *Columbus Dispatch*, July 16, 2005.

54. See, e.g., Farhad Manjoo, "Was the 2004 Election Stolen? No," http://www.salon.com (making this argument and quoting William Anthony).

55. http://www.franklincountyohio.gov/commissioners/budget.

56. Jerry L. Mashaw, "Structuring a "Dense Complexity": Accountability and the Project of Administrative Law," *Issues in Legal Scholarship*, March 2005, http://www.bepress.com/ils/iss6.art4.

57. Cass Sunstein and others, for instance, have written about the pressures of conformity upon individuals. Cass R. Sunstein, *Why Societies Need Dissent* (Cambridge: Harvard University Press, 2003). One of the results of conformity is a decision-making "cascade" (Sunstein, 10–11). If one set of decision makers or "early movers" converges on a particular option, subsequent decision makers—influenced by the agreement of the first movers—make the same choice even if they would not have reached such a decision independently (Sunstein, 10–11, defining conformity and cascades). Sunstein also explains both why reasonable people rely on the decisions of first movers and why this tendency sometimes has unfortunate consequences (54–73).

58. The global polity "consists of much more than a 'system of states' or 'world economy' or 'international system.' Rather, the global environment is a sea teaming with a great variety of social units—states and their associated polities, military alliances, business enterprises, social movements, terrorists, political activists, nongovernmental organizations—all of which may be involved in relations with the polity." John Boli, "Sovereignty from a World Polity Perspective," in *Problematic Sovereignty: Contested Rules and Political Possibilities*, ed. Stephen D. Krasner (New York: Columbia University Press, 2001), 59–60. For a helpful survey of this literature, see John W. Meyer, "The World Polity and the Authority of the Nation-States," in *Studies of the Modern World-System*, ed. Albert Bergesen (New York: Academic Press, 1980); John W. Meyer, John Boli, George M. Thomas, and Francisco O. Ramirez, "World Society and the Nation-State," 103 *American Journal of Sociology* 144 (1997); Martha Finnemore, "Norms, Culture, and World Politics: Insights from Sociology's Institutionalism," 50 *International Organization* 325 (1996); Gili Drori, John W. Meyer, and Hokyu Hwang, eds., *Globalization and Organization: World Society and Organizational Change* (New York: Oxford University Press, 2006). For a general introduction to the social science behind the global polity literature, see W. Richard Scott, *Institutions and Organizations*, 2nd ed. (Thousand Oaks, Calif.: Sage, 2001). Ryan Goodman and Derek Jinks have led the way in connecting this literature to legal

scholarship and exploring its potential ramifications for international law, particularly human rights law. See Ryan Goodman and Derek Jinks, "Towards an Institutional Theory of Sovereignty," 55 *Stanford Law Review* 1749 (2003); Ryan Goodman and Derek Jinks, "How to Influence States: Socialization and International Human Rights Law," 54 *Duke Law Journal* 621 (2004).

59. Gili Drori, John W. Meyer, Francisco O. Ramirez, and Evan Schofer, *Science in the Modern World Polity: Institutionalization and Globalization* (Stanford, Calif.: Stanford University Press, 2003), ix. For instance, nation-states deploy similar record-keeping systems and mandate mass education in school systems using similar curricula and administrative structures. Isomorphism and decoupling have been found in "constitutional forms emphasizing both state power and individual rights, mass schooling systems organized around a fairly standard curriculum, rationalized economic and demographic record keeping and date systems, antinatalist population control policies intended to enhance national development, formally equalized female states and rights, expanded human rights in general, expansive environmental policies, development-oriented economic policy, universalistic welfare systems, standard definitions of disease and health care and even some basic demographic variables." See Meyer et al., "World Society and the Nation-State, 152–53. See also David John Frank, Suk-Ying Wong, John W. Meyer, and Francisco O. Ramirez, "What Counts as History: A Cross-National and Longitudinal Study of University Curricula," 44 *Comparative Education Review* 29 (2000); John W. Meyer, "The Changing Cultural Content of World Society," in *State/Culture: State-Formation after the Cultural Turn*, ed. George Steinmetz (Ithaca, N.Y.: Cornell University Press, 1999); Karen Bradley and Francisco O. Ramirez, "World Polity Promotion of Gender Parity: Women's Share of Higher Education, 1965–85," 11 *Research in Sociology of Education and Socialization* 63 (1996).

60. See Finnemore, "Norms, Culture, and World Politics," 336–37. Similarly, the enrollment of women in institutions of higher education, for example, increased around the world at roughly the same rate and at about the same time in Western and non-Western countries. See Bradley and Ramirez, "World Polity Promotion."

61. Martha Finnemore, "International Organizations as Teachers of Norms: The United Nations Educational, Scientific, and Cultural Organization and Science Policy," 47 *International Organization* 567, 593 (1993).

62. See, e.g., Jack L. Walker, "The Diffusion of Innovations among the American States," 63 *American Political Science Review* 880 (1969); Virginia Gray, "Innovation in the States: A Diffusion Study," 67 *American Political Science Review* 1174 (1973).

63. This literature is vast, so what follows is only a sampling drawn primarily from the work of sociologists and political scientists. See, e.g., Frances Stokes Berry and William D. Berry, "State Lottery Adoptions as Policy Innovations: An Event History Analysis," 84 *American Political Science Review* 395 (1990); Frances Stokes Berry and William D. Berry, "Tax Innovation in the States: Capitalizing on Political Opportunity," 36 *American Journal of Political Science* 715 (1992); Frances Stokes Berry and William D. Berry, "Innovation and Diffusion Models in Policy Research," in *Theories of the Policy Process*, ed. Paul A. Sabatier (Boulder, Colo.: Westview Press, 1999); Karen Mossberger, *The Politics of Ideas and the Spread of Enterprise Zones* (Washington, D.C.: Georgetown University Press, 2000); Henry R. Glick, *The Right to Die: Policy Innovation and Its Consequences* (New York: Columbia University Press, 1992); Michael Mintrom, "Policy Entrepreneurs and the Diffusion of Innovation," 41 *American Journal of Political Science* 738 (1997); Michael Mintrom and Sandra Vergari, "Policy Networks and Innovation Diffusion: The Case of State Education Reforms," 60 *Journal of Politics* 126 (1998); Andrew Karch, *Democratic Laboratories: Policy Diffusion among the American States* (Ann Arbor: University of Michigan Press, 2007); Anne Schneider and Helen Ingram, "Systematically Pitching Ideas: A Comparative Approach to Policy Design," 8 *Journal of Public Policy* 61, 62 (1988); Richard Rose, *Lesson-Drawing in Public Policy: A Guide to Learning across Time and Space* (Chatham, N.J.: Chatham House, 1993); David L. Weimer, "The Current State of Design Craft: Borrowing, Tinkering, and Problem Solving," 55 *Public Administration Review* 110 (1993); Steven J. Balla, "Interstate Professional Associations and the Diffusion of Policy Innovations," 29 *American Politics Research* 221 (2001); Harold Wolman and Ed Page, "Policy Transfer among Local Governments: An Information-Theory Approach, 15 *Governance* 477, 496–98 (2002). For a critical take on some of this work, see Christopher Z. Mooney, "Modeling Regional Effects on State Policy Diffusion," 54 *Political Research Quarterly* 103 (2001) (questioning whether regional effects on diffusion are as pronounced as prior work has suggested). For examination of interstate diffusion among European Union states and Canadian provinces, see

Katerina Linos, "When Do Policy Innovations Spread? Lessons for Advocates of Line Drawing," 199 *Harvard Law Review* 1467 (2006); Katerina Linos, "How Can International Organizations Shape National Welfare States? Evidence from Compliance with European Union Directives," 40 *Comparative Political Studies* 547 (2007); James M. Luz, "Emulation and Policy Adoptions in Canadian Provinces," 22 *Canadian Journal of Political Studies* 147 (1989); Dale H. Pole, "The Diffusion of Legislation among Canadian Provinces: A Statistical Analysis," 9 *Canadian Journal of Political Studies* 605 (1976). For a survey of the literature on diffusion among nonstate organizations, see David Strang and Sarah A. Soule, "Diffusion in Organizations and Social Movements: From Hybrid Corn to Poison Pills," 24 *Annual Review of Sociology* 265 (1998). As one of the earliest pieces in the field explains, policy diffusion takes place within "a national system of emulation and competition" (Walker, "Diffusion of Innovations," 898). A network that "links together the centers of research and generation of new ideas, national associations of professional administrators, interest groups, and voluntary associations" helps establish "a set of norms or national standards for proper administration" (898).

64. Karch, *Democratic Laboratories*, 2–3.

65. Karch, *Democratic Laboratories*, 7–8.

66. A recent survey indicates that 60 percent of local officials do not belong to a national professional association, and one-quarter of local officials do not belong to any professional association. Eric A. Fischer and Kevin J. Coleman, "Election Reform and Local Election Officials: Results of Two National Surveys," *Congressional Research Service Report for Congress*, RL-34363, February 7, 2008, 5–6.

67. Grayson, interview; Goldman, interview; interview with anonymous election official. It is worth noting that these organizations lack the resources they need to provide such broad services to their members. The National Association of Secretaries of State, for instance, has an extraordinarily small staff and has accomplished an impressive amount with the staff it possesses.

68. Interview with Leslie Reynolds, December 11, 2007.

69. Interview with Ray Martinez, January 24, 2008.

70. Anonymous interview, April 15, 2008.

71. Smith, interview.

72. Linos, "When Do Policy Innovations Spread?" 1473; Strang and Soule, "Diffusion in Organizations," 274–75.

73. Joyce, interview.

74. Nelson, interview.

75. Nelson, interview.

76. Karch, *Democratic Laboratories*, 8. This is, to be sure, not a conclusion reached only by political scientists. Sociologists Harold Wolman and Ed Page, for instance, have reached a similar conclusion. Harold Wolman and Edward Page, "Policy Transfers among Local Governments," 15 *Governance* 477, 498 (2002).

77. Balla, "Interstate Professional Associations"; Karch, *Democratic Laboratories*, 105–43. For work in sociology exploring similar themes in the context of private institutions, see, e.g., Lauren B. Edelman, Christopher Uggen, and Howard S. Erlanger, "The Endogeneity of Legal Regulation: Grievance Procedures as Rational Myth," 105 *American Journal of Sociology* 406 (1999); Lauren Edelman, "Legal Environments and Organizational Governance: The Expansion of Due Process in the Workplace," 95 *American Journal of Sociology* 1401 (1999).

78. Mintrom, "Policy Entrepreneurs"; Mintrom and Vergari, "Policy Networks."

79. Karch, *Democratic Laboratories.*

80. Karch, *Democratic Laboratories*, 31.

81. Karch, *Democratic Laboratories*, 8.

82. Karch, *Democratic Laboratories*, 9.

83. Greene, interview.

CHAPTER 4: IS THE GAME WORTH THE CANDLE?

1. Stein Ringen, *What Democracy Is For: On Freedom and Moral Government* 283 (Princeton, N.J.: Princeton University Press, 2007).

2. Esty, interview.

3. Indeed, this is true of both of the democracy indexes that exist—the "Index of democracy" put out by the *Economist*, www.economist.com/media/DEMOCRACY_INDEX_2007_v3.pdf, and the "Democracy Index" put out by Fair Vote, http://www.fairvote.org/?page=729.

4. Esty, interview.

5. Esty, interview.

6. Angell, *Once More around the Park*, 4.

7. Interview with David Roodman, February 1, 2008.

8. Roodman, "Building and Running an Index." 2

9. Ringen, *What Democracy Is For*, 284.

10. Michael Maslin, cartoon, *New Yorker* July 23, 2001.

11. Greene, interview.

12. Ringen, *What Democracy Is For*, 284.

13. Yale Center for Environmental Law and Policy and CIESIN, *EPI Report*, 285.

14. Esty, interview.

15. Roodman, interview.

16. Roodman, interview.

17. Thanks to Christine Jolls for offering this suggestion.

18. There is, needless to say, a cost to change. As David Roodman, an architect of the Commitment to Development Index, observes, when an Index "jump[s] from year to year," it undermines the Index's ability to serve as a "policy metric." Nonetheless, Roodman argues—correctly, in my view—"the benefits of public learning—a more credible Index—will outweigh the costs provided that the Index methodology stabilizes in due course." Roodman, "Building and Running an Index," 8.

19. Esty, presentation at Designing a Democracy Index Conference.

20. Roodman, "Building and Running an Index," 12.

21. Ringen, *What Democracy Is For*, 284.

22. Oxford's Stein Ringen frames the question similarly but offers a different answer. He argues that the decision whether to rank depends on whether one wants to "guide decisionmakers towards good decisions" or "assist towards a rational political process" (*What Democracy Is For*, 285). In his view, these categories boil down to "measurement" and "social reporting" (286). When decision makers just need information about facts on the ground in order to decide, indexing is a sensible strategy. But, argues Ringen, when the issue at stake involves "political, normative, or moral questions," indexing improperly short-circuits the deliberative process (285–86).

23. For the substantive pros and cons of the *U.S. News & World Report* rankings, with most people firmly in the con camp, compare, e.g., Ronald G. Ehrenberg, "Method or Madness: Inside the *U.S. News & World Report* Rankings," 29 *Journal of College Admission* 29 (2005); Stephen Klein and Laura Hamilton, "The Validity of the *U.S. News & World Report* Ranking of ABA Law Schools," report commissioned by the American Association of Law Schools, February 18, 1998, http://www.aals.org/reports/validity.html; Shuky Ehrenberg, "A Question

of Rank: An Empirical Investigation into Law School Rank Maximizing Strategies, with a Focus on Admissions Decisions," 10, http://papers.ssrn.com/sol3/papers.cfm?abstract_id=976200; and Michael Sauder and Ryan Lancaster, "Do Rankings Matter? The Effects of *U.S. News & World Report* Rankings on the Admissions Process of Law Schools," 40 *Law and Society Review* 105, 106 (2006); with Mitchell Berger, "Why the *U.S. News and World Report* Law School Rankings Are Both Useful and Important," 51 *Journal of Legal Education* 487 (2001); and "Indiana University School of Law 2005 Symposium on the Next Generation of Law School Rankings," 81 *Indiana Law Journal* 1 (2006). It is worth noting that some critics of the *U.S. News & World Report* rankings quarrel with its methodology, but not the idea of ranking itself. For instance, Brian Leiter, one of the most trenchant critics, believes that a good ranking is possible. See "Brian Leiter's Law School Rankings," http://www.leiterrankings.com/.

24. Alex Wellen, "The $8.78 Million Maneuver," *New York Times*, July 31, 2005.

25. Wellen, "The $8.78 Million Maneuver."

26. Wellen, "The $8.78 Million Maneuver."

27. Wellen, "The $8.78 Million Maneuver."

28. For a useful analysis of this problem, see Esty and Rushing, *Governing by the Numbers*, 38.

29. Joyce, interview.

30. It is worth noting that this requirement has generated a good deal of debate and controversy among corporations and academics. Congress would have to think hard about the lessons learned from Sarbanes-Oxley before taking this path.

31. Esty, interview.

32. Megan Greenfield, "The People's Revenge," *Washington Post*, June 14, 1978, A27.

CHAPTER 5: GETTING FROM HERE TO THERE IN MINIATURE

1. Ohio Rev. Code § 3501.35.

2. Mansky, interview, May 6, 2008.

3. Damschroder, interview.

4. Interview with anonymous reformer, January 8, 2008.

5. Andrew Gumbel, "Connie [*sic*] McCormack: 3rd Degree," *Los Angeles City Beat*, http://www.lacitybeat.com/article.php?id=942&IssueNum=51; Andrew

Gumbel, "Conny's Final Ballot," *Los Angles City Beat*, http://www.lacitybeat.com/article.php?id=6118&IssueNum=222.

6. See, e.g., Robert F. Kennedy, Jr., "Was the 2004 Election Stolen?" *Rolling Stone Magazine*, June 1, 2006.

7. Thomas Mann, Pew Journalists Forum, December 10, 2007, Washington, D.C.

8. Mark Niquette, "Franklin County Elections Chief to Lead Statewide Group," *Columbus Dispatch*, March 13, 2007.

9. Interview with Tammy Patrick, June 5, 2008.

10. Dean C. Logan, Memorandum, Preliminary Findings and Analysis of Sample Set of Non-partisan Ballots Cast in the February 5, 2008 Presidential Primary Election, February 11, 2008.

11. Email from Kim Alexander to Heather Gerken, June 30, 2008.

12. Thanks to Steve Weir for letting me use this phrase.

13. Goldman, interview.

14. Martinez, interview.

15. "Tokaji and Hall, "Money for Data."

16. Brunner, interview.

17. Some privately funded studies have large sample sizes but classify voters by region, not by state or locality. Others classify voters by state but don't survey enough voters within each state or locality to offer trustworthy samples. Still other studies just don't ask the right questions. With the support of political scientists and foundations, however, it is possible to imagine correcting these problems in order to piggyback on existing research.

18. I borrow the *Field of Dreams* reference from Edward B. Foley, "A Model Court for Contested Elections (or the 'Field of Dreams' Approach to Election Law Reform)," http://moritzlaw.osu.edu/electionlaw/comments/articles.php?ID=157.

19. Deborah Hastings, "Problems, Funding Plague Voting Panel," Associated Press, June 23, 2008.

20. Martinez, interview.

21. Martinez, interview.

22. For an extended analysis of deliberation and its role in contemporary politics, see Amy Gutmann and Dennis Thompson, *Democracy and Disagreement* (Cambridge: Belknap Press of Harvard University Press, 1996).

23. I make this argument in extended form in "Double-Edged Sword of Independence."

24. http://www.csuchico.edu/econ/old/links/econhumor.html.

25. Thanks to Doug Chapin and Charles Stewart for formulating the issue this way.

26. Charles Stewart, Data for Democracy Conference, Pew Center on the States, May 12–13, 2008.

27. Eric Fischer, Data for Democracy Conference, Pew Center on the States, May 12–13, 2008.

28. Smith, interview.

29. Murphy, interview.

30. Hernando de Soto, *The Mystery of Capital: Why Capitalism Triumphs in the West and Fails Everywhere Else* (New York: Basic Books, 2000), 28.

31. For information on Nielsen families, see http://www.nielsenmedia.com/nc/portal/site/Public/. Many thanks to David Schleicher for the great analogy.

32. Stewart, "Measuring the Improvement," 7.

33. The 2006 Cooperative Congressional Election Study (CCES), an opt-in Internet-based survey put together by several universities, already asks people how long they stood in line and whether they encountered any problems in registering to vote.

34. Stewart, "Measuring the Improvement," 12–13.

CONCLUSION: GETTING FROM "HERE TO THERE" REDUX

1. David Brooks, "Thoroughly Modern Do-Gooders," op-ed, *New York Times*, March 21, 2008. For more systemic studies, see David Bornstein, *How to Change the World: Social Entrepreneurs and the Power of New Ideas* (New York: Oxford University Press, 2004); Charles Leadbetter, *The Rise of the Social Entrepreneur* (London: Demos, 1997); and Johanna Mair et al., eds., *Social Entrepreneurship* (New York: Palgrave Macmillan, 2006).

AFTERWORD

1. 153 Cong. Rec. S 2503 (2007).

Index